E. A. (Ezra Adams) Stafford

The need of minstrelsy: and other sermons

E. A. (Ezra Adams) Stafford

The need of minstrelsy: and other sermons

ISBN/EAN: 9783743451520

Manufactured in Europe, USA, Canada, Australia, Japa

Cover: Foto ©Thomas Meinert / pixelio.de

Manufactured and distributed by brebook publishing software (www.brebook.com)

E. A. (Ezra Adams) Stafford

The need of minstrelsy: and other sermons

THE NEED OF MINSTRELSY:

AND OTHER SERMONS.

MEMORIAL VOLUME

OF THE LATE

REV. E. A. STAFFORD, D.D., LL.D.

WITH INTRODUCTION

By REV. D. G. SUTHERLAND, D.D., LL.B.

TORONTO:

WILLIAM BRIGGS,

WESLEY BUILDINGS.

MONTREAL: C. W. COATES.   HALIFAX: S. F. HUESTIS.

1892

CARL RIENZI (?) M D

INTRODUCTION.

W HEN a man of marked individuality and of wide-
spread fame and influence passes away, there is
a laudable desire on the part, not only of his friends, but
of the public generally, to possess some suitable and abiding memorial of his life and labors. Such a man was the
Rev. Ezra A. Stafford, D.D., LL.D., and such a memorial
is this volume of sermons intended to be.

Dr. Stafford had won to himself hosts of friends and
admirers, to whom his unexpected death was a cause of
deepest sorrow. This volume can by no means fill the
void, but amid the wearing processes of time will serve to
keep alive the thoughts and teaching of one who charmed
so many by his words. The task of selecting from amid
the mass of material left has been a difficult one. Some
of his most celebrated and characteristic sermons are not
fully written out, and had to be laid aside; moreover,
the preacher was in the habit of introducing into those
more fully prepared living illustrations and modes of

expression, of which no record remains. One might also as well seek to call back the fragrance of last year's flower as attempt to depict in words the quaint but effective look and intonation which gave force and pungency to his utterances. Nearly all the sermons included in this volume, however, were evidently favorites of the author, and were preached in most of his leading appointments. Some have been specially asked for by friends. From their perusal no doubt a very fair idea will be obtained of the author's modes of thought. Portions of them will come back to loving hearts like well-remembered strains of music. No one will read them without having a higher idea of his tender sympathy with human woes, and his loving relations to Christ Jesus and all mankind.

D. G. S.

CONTENTS.

CONTENTS.

CONTENTS.

In Memoriam.

EZRA ADAMS STAFFORD first saw the light of day on a farm in the township of Southwold, county of Elgin, in what was then called Upper Canada, on the 9th of September, 1839. He was one of a family of eleven children, and there was nothing in his early years to distinguish him from other boys of his age. He went to school, and assisted every morning and evening in feeding the cattle and horses, and in the summer time took his fair share of work in the hay and harvest fields. That early experience was one of life's best training-schools in habits of industry and adaptability. Isolated as it was, it was not without its simple pleasures. In days when railroads were unknown, and the modern excursion unthought of, it was quite an event in this farmer boy's life to drive to Port Stanley on a load of grain, or to visit the adjacent village on training-day, when the farmers and their sons held their annual muster and received a slight drill in military steps. At a very early period, young Ezra showed that independence of spirit

which always characterized him. When sixteen
years of age he obtained a certificate to teach, and
soon afterwards was placed in charge of a district
school, beginning thus early to provide for his own
living and to influence and shape the lives of others.

It was while teaching school, and in the twentieth
year of his age, that he passed through that religious experience which was the crisis of his life, and
the impulse to all the noble pursuits and attainments, the toils and successes of later years. It was
to him not only revelation, but revolution. In the
diary of the late Meredith Conn, the venerable
backwoods class-leader of sainted memory, is an ex-
tended reference to this important event, under the
date of Dec. 10th, 1859. The young teacher had
been working for a short time in the Sabbath
School, and attending a few meetings of the class,
when he suddenly broke down under the conviction
of guilt and sin. He sought and found the knowledge of pardon and salvation. His leader impressed
upon him the duty of consecrating his talents to the
Lord, and urged him to prepare for the work of the
ministry. He was at length persuaded to officiate
in the absence of the pastor, and preached "two excellent sermons," one in the Union chapel, Southwold, and the other in the chapel at Tyrconnel. Soon

afterwards he is found aiding the pastor in a pro-
tracted service, where "in the space of three weeks
forty sinners are converted to God."

In the year 1860, he was admitted on probation
for the ministry of the Wesleyan Methodist Church,
and was ordained in 1864. During that time he
spent one year at Victoria College, where his mind
received a scholastic bent and inspiration which
awakened its noblest faculties and loftiest aspirations. The first few years of his ministry were in
the western part of Ontario, where he was looked
upon as a young man of wonderful gifts, destined
to occupy a high place in the Church. It was not,
however, until 1874, that he came prominently
before the public, when he received an appointment
to Dominion Square Church, Montreal, a position
which he afterwards held for a second term. Between these two terms he spent three years in
charge of the Dominion Methodist Church at
Ottawa, where he obtained great fame and exercised
wide influence among the legislators of the land.

In 1883 he was transferred to the city of Winni-
peg for two years, whence he came, in 1885, to
Toronto, serving there as pastor of the Metropolitan
and Sherbourne Street Churches successively—positions demanding the choicest talents and most

earnest devotion to duty. His last charge was over
the Centenary Church, Hamilton, where, after a
brief service of five months, his bright spirit passed
home to receive its glorious reward.

During his ministerial career, he was the recipient
of many honors at the hands of his brethren. He
was elected President of the Montreal, Manitoba and
Toronto Conferences respectively, and was five times
a member of the General Conference of the Methodist
Church. His voice was frequently heard in the
discussion of most important questions. In 1886 he
was appointed to the honorable post of representing Canadian Methodism before the General
Conference of the Methodist Episcopal Church of
the United States. This position he filled to the
great satisfaction of all parties. His address before
the immense gathering in the Metropolitan Opera
House received great praise from men highly distinguished for their public success. The occasion
was a trying one, but the speaker rose to its demands. Nor were scholastic honors wanting in his
career. He took in course at Victoria University
the degrees of Bachelor of Arts and of Laws, and he
was also honored with the Doctorate in Divinity. In
1886 he received, after examination before his *Alma
Mater*, the degree of Doctor of Laws.

Dr. Stafford was always a close and diligent student. His mind was of a keen, enquiring turn, eagerly entering into all fields of knowledge. He early learned to think for himself. He would not bow to any idol the world of philosophy or theology had set up, or accept any creed or dogma simply because his text-books taught it. It is possible that at times he went to extremes in asserting his independence of thought. He had a hatred of shams and an inveterate dislike to ruts. This brought from him many a keen shaft of wit and much quiet, good-natured sarcasm. His public discourses and private conversations were marked by a freshness and originality that were the delight of young and old, of students and men of the world. The quaintness of his illustrations and constant reference to the common events of life were attractive to both saint and sinner. He made the whole world of nature and of men tributary to his work. This was manifest even in life's closing hours. Some flowers having been laid upon his bed, he picked up one and soliloquized, "The fragrance of a flower— the fragrance of a life—the fragrance of Christ's life!"

The natural kindness and tenderness of his heart won many to him. His sympathies were quickly aroused, and he was in touch with the brotherhood

of men. "He was an earnest, true and sincere
friend," writes an associate of many years, "incapable of doing anything but what was high and noble."

Beside the attachment of many valued friends, he
twice won to himself the love and life of woman to
brighten his home and gladden his toils. His first
wife, Miss Eliza H. Hurlburt, daughter of Rev.
Thomas Hurlburt, was taken to the better world in
1875. His second wife, Miss Caroline C. Baird, of
Montreal, was united to him in 1876, and had the
melancholy satisfaction of helping to soothe his
sufferings in his last painful illness. A son and a
daughter by the first union, and a son by the second,
deeply mourn the loss of a loving father.

A fuller idea of his character may be gathered from
the eloquent words of John W. Dowd, Esq., at the
memorial service in the Sherbourne Street Church,
Toronto, and other intimate friends:

"Dr. Stafford was unique. His personality was
all his own. He was himself, and always refused
to be the copy of anybody else. He had no reverence for authority that would not bear the search-
lights of investigation. He laid all sources of
knowledge under tribute. He was *greedy* of knowing. He challenged everything, but tenaciously and
reverently held fast to what he believed to be good.

There was no pretence in his nature. He was simplicity itself. He hated shams and humbugs with a holy hatred. I do not believe he ever consciously did a mean act, and I never knew him to be angry except at the meanness of others. With him there was no assumption of superiority or perfection. He was full of charity for the man who made mistakes, evidently believing that the man who made no mistakes never made anything. While his words were hot and scorching for the man who did wrong— intending to do wrong—his sympathy was as broad as human needs and as deep as human misery. He would feed a tramp, beguile from him his story, and thus learn a lesson to teach his fellow-man. He would lift the drunkard from the gutter, and with his arm placed kindly about him endeavor to steady his feet to walk the way of life.

"To listen to his teaching—for his preaching was always teaching—was in itself an education. It was the delight of his life to solve difficulties, and make dark things plain to his people. He was no oracle. He did not *pretend* to know ; but when he was sure, he was a great persuader of men.

"Who that ever heard can forget his prayers. They were sacred poems lifting the worshippers up through the shining stars to the very gates of the

celestial city. Those prayers were a great revealer
of the man.

"How plain and simple was his last Sunday at
Sherbourne Street; and how touching his last request
for remembrance : ' When you lift your eyes to the
friendly stars, will you sometimes think of me !' "

His friend, Mr. John Donagh, writes of him : "He
had a keen sense of humor, and could always see,
and seldom could resist the temptation to present the
funny side of the subject of conversation. He was
a master of sarcasm, and was marvellously fluent in
the use of quaint and striking phrases. He often
illustrated his sermons with what might be called a
novelette, and had the art of a Dickens in clothing
his characters with flesh and blood, and making
them speak the truths he wished to convey.

"He loved to present the Lord Jesus as 'the one
who was tempted in all points like as we are,' and
who 'is touched with the feeling of our infirmi-
ties.' To his view, God was always the loving
Father, holding the door of mercy wide open and
standing with outstretched arms to welcome the
returning sinner."

The Rev. Dr. Withrow, in the *Methodist Maga-
zine*, writes of him : "The great religious, social and
economic questions of the times throbbed in his

breast and brain. He felt a keen sympathy with the toiling masses. He often spoke of the dislocated relations of society, and hoped and labored for its re-organization on the basis of the golden rule. He believed that much of the sin, and suffering and sorrow, on which the pitying eye of God looks down, was largely the result of physical environment."

His sympathy overleaped denominational barriers. He longed for the union of Christian bodies under the standard of Christian charity and liberty. " It has always been my ambition," he said, a few hours before death, " to have the same love in my heart as brought the Saviour from such a distance to die for me. I have had a measure of that love, and consequently I feel enmity to no one. That love has made everything pure to me." He was an earnest promoter of the union of the various Methodist bodies in Canada, and aided much in arranging the basis of union.

Had time and opportunity been given him, he would have become a successful worker in the literary world. He has left behind him tokens of his skill in his published articles on " Voltaire and John Wesley"; " Robert Elsmere "; " My Friend, the Tramp"; " The Indebtedness of Christianity to Free Thought"; The Unchurched Masses ";

2

"The Common Parentage of the Human Race"; in
his lectures on "Individuality in Woman"; "The
Universal Boy"; "Modes of Culture Out of
School"; "Get Your Money's Worth"; in his essay
on "Ecclesiastical Law"; in his book of poems
entitled, "Recreations"; and in his works, "The
Guiding Hand," dealing with the subject of Divine
Guidance; and "The United Church."

His last illness was comparatively short, and his
end came unexpectedly. For months he had suffered
from periodical pains in the head, but the cause of
his death could not be determined until a post-mor-
tem examination revealed the existence of a large
tumor in the brain. In spite of cerebral pain and
failing strength, he continued his pulpit work until
within five weeks of his decease. His will-power
often sustained him and compelled him to face
heavy tasks, when his physical system was crying
out for rest. A trip to the Bahama Islands for rest
and change was planned, but it was not to be.
Physical weakness drove him to his bed; yet while
sufficient strength remained he delighted in the
visits of friends, and they were welcomed with the
old familiar smile and pleasant words. As he
recognized the approaching shadows of death he
gave no sign of shrinking. Looking up with a smile

of pleasure after the reading of the twenty-third Psalm, he said, "That is good ; I am going to dwell in my Father's house." His gentleness under suffering was very touching, and his natural playfulness repeatedly asserted itself. His mind was kept in perfect peace. Once, after hearing " Jesus, Lover of My Soul" sung, he remarked, "That is all I have tc depend upon," and enlarged upon the beauty and richness of the hymn, and upon the tender love of Christ. When that other familiar hymn of Toplady's, " Rock of Ages, Cleft for Me," was sung, he cried, " What a reality that is to me !"

He was especially fond of the hymn, " All Hail the Power of Jesus' Name," and when it was being sung shortly before his death he joined in the song, and at the last verse his face partook of almost unearthly brightness as he cried, " Oh, if you could only see the rapture that I see !" ' The scene will never be forgotten by those that stood by.

There is something very touching in his last intelligent act. Taking a pencil in his weak fingers he began to write a few words to his congregation on the blank pages of a book. The letters were very trembling and are read with difficulty. So far as they can be made out they read thus : " My beloved people, my thoughts have been that I might think eminently suitable."

On Monday, December 21st, 1891, Ezra A. Stafford, the admired and beloved of thousands, "fell asleep in Jesus," at the age of 52. A solemn memorial service was held at the Centenary Church, Hamilton, on December 24th, attended by a large gathering of friends and brethren in the ministry. And by request a funeral sermon was preached by the writer, as chairman of the Hamilton District, on the following Sunday evening. A similar memorial service was also held at Sherbourne Street Church, Toronto, and another at the Dominion Square Church, Montreal, whither the body was taken for interment, and in whose God's-acre it now lies awaiting the dawning of the resurrection morn.

We close with a brief extract from Mr. J. W. Bengough's beautiful tribute to his memory :—

" A Sabbath sunlight round the tall, lithe form,
Which shrined a soul wide as the human race,
That looked abroad with sad and gentle eyes,
Anon with humor kindling, yet which flashed
At times the lightning of a righteous wrath ;
And spoke, through lips that wore a genial smile,
The homely phrase that sent an old, old truth
Upon its errand, looking almost new.

    .   .   .   .
Bereavèd Methodism kneels and weeps
At Stafford's tomb, but not in solitude.
Beside her all her sister churches bend ;
Creeds count for nought ; this plain dead preacher here
Was great enough to love and reverence each,
And so is mourned by all."

                                        D. G. S.

THE NEED OF MINSTRELSY.

"Now bring me a minstrel. And it came to pass when the minstrel played, that the hand of the Lord came upon him."
2 Kings iii. 15.

THREE kings were with their armies in a region where there was no water. They could do nothing. War was out of the question. They were already vanquished, before a blow was struck, if relief in this particular were not secured. The best man among them turned their thoughts to the Lord, as their only hope. So the three kings went down together to Elisha, the prophet of the Lord. They found the prophet, but he was not in the spirit of his highest work. Either because of the badness of two of the kings especially, who had come to consult him, or from some cause in himself or surroundings (of this we can have no certain knowledge), he was not prepared at once with that elevated spirit of foresight, which would enable him to minister suitably to the occasion. So he asked that a minstrel be called, and while he played he felt the hand of the Lord come upon him.

Probably his unreadiness was due to the fact that

prophecies were generally put in the form of poetry, and the minstrel's music enabled him the more easily to fall into the rude measure which the prophets generally employed. In the same way Moses, and Miriam, and Nathan, and Elijah, and David, and Isaiah, and Jeremiah, burst out into prophetic language only at certain times, not always; and that was when the prophetic rapture took possession of their souls.

We are not at present interested in the prophecy Elisha uttered on this occasion. The kings and their armies received an abundant supply of water and returned victorious.

That to which we wish now to turn your thoughts, is the need of minstrelsy in the case of Elisha, to prepare him for the highest form of service to God and men; and from this by an easy step we pass to the fact that all good men sometimes get out of the spirit of their true work for God. There are times when they are not ready to enter upon the highest forms of service to God and men. We will now examine:

I. The causes why Christian people sometimes are not in the spirit of true Christian labor.

II. What minstrelsy is needful to bring upon them again the hand of the Lord.

I. The causes.

1. One cause of this declension in power may be bad health. Sickness may always claim the supporting grace of God, and always gets it when it is

asked ; but all the same, the great surging waves of pain that attend some conditions of the body, or the sunken weariness of aimless existence that men feel at other times when their energies are exhausted, is favorable neither to high emotion, nor to earnest endeavor.

Above all a condition of half health and half sickness, attended with great nervous irritability, will give a person a most unsatisfactory religious experience. He will seem to have shown temper when his reason and feeling both tell him that he is not angry. His performance of duty seems to reach so low a standard that he grows morbid in self-reproach. He is unhappy within himself, and beyond doubt he is out of tune for the highest form of Christian duty.

And this is the condition the year through, of many men of business who spend so many hours in an office where the sun never shone, that they themselves forget how to shine. The objects therein are printed on their minds as a hideous nightmare, and ledgers, and charts, and chairs and desks, know their thoughts better than anything else on earth.

This is the state of very many excellent women whose motherhood commands so much of their attention that they forget how once their life did, and might again, prove warmth and benediction to all they touch.

The minstrelsy he needs is thorough rest and change. If possible let him go where breezes mur-

mur, and brooks gurgle, and waves dash, and birds
sing, and listen to the great anthem of the world's
unwritten music, and bathe in undiluted, undefiled
sunshine; let him forget for a time that his church
has any work to perform, and even that other men
have souls to save, and feel the relaxation that comes
from knowing that God allows him to be just naturally simply happy, then the hand of the Lord would
come upon him and he would return to his church
and labor for God with happiness to himself and
blessing to all.

2. Another cause of this decline in power is other
people's influence upon us. I stood last summer
charmed and enchained for a long time at a place
on the seashore, where a great cave had been cut
out, and it swept around in a fair semi-circular
form, and in all its extent there rose up, receding
back like the ascending rows of seats in an amphi-
theatre, a gentle slope from low tide mark to the
top a hundred feet or more. When I stood there
the tide was coming in, and the sea was high, and
the waves swept like a great stroke of almighty
power clear up to the highest line. Then as they
receded, and laid the beautiful slope bare for seventy
feet down, more than a million stones from the
size of an acorn and upwards were jostled against
each other and went hurrying down with a rattling
noise as of a hundred hail storms all in one, each
greater than the greatest I ever witnessed. Every
one of those stones was polished to its highest

capacity. There was not a sharp corner to be found on one of them. Standing there I thought in how small a degree any person determines the form or style of his own character. "The world is so full of other folks."

"I am! How little more I know!" We maintain an identity because we are born singly and must die alone; business and social life and church influences lift and whirl and toss us, and wear upon us, and men throw themselves against everything in us that is peculiar and distinctive, and try to break it up, and it is only the life in us that keeps us from falling into a dull, monotonous uniformity like the stones on the beach; for I noticed that they were almost all oval in circumference and somewhat flattened. And so men get somewhat flat if they do not resist the moulding influence of society.

Now, is it remarkable that a man's religious life should be much affected by other people? Most people are not like Christ. They are not spiritual in mind. I do not say that most people do not go to church, or that they are not members of the church. But there are many who are members of churches because it is fashionable and respectable. For the same reason in Turkey, they would be Mohammedans; in India, Buddhists; in China, they would follow Confucius. They are not Christians through love of Christ. They do not like a religion with any cross in it, that teaches the duty of self-denial, except of those things which, if they

should do, they would have to go to jail, or that
does not think better of sin if it bears an inoffensive
name, and if it dresses well, and is polite, and lives
in a grand house in expensive style. In short, their
religion is an effort to get to heaven on the qualification of worldly respectability. The easy religion,
which denies its professor no pleasure, will hang
before his eye as a very beautiful picture, appealing
to every selfish element in his nature, which at any
time he keeps under restraint only by great watch-
fulness. Now, whenever any person is trying, like
Elisha, to do true work for God, to be a spiritual,
working Christian, he will find his zeal depressed by
contact with Christians of this worldly stamp. Perhaps his earnestness will be called hypocrisy. His
motives will probably be misrepresented, or at least
they will be misunderstood.

If he is a poor man his character will be constantly affected by other people's vaunting display
of their wealth, and he will be stung by the world's
habit of estimating manhood by its ability to bring
together and invest money. Above all, the pomp of
numbers, the stateliness of the multitude, bewilders
the imagination of men generally.

And so, without knowing it, without intending it,
one whom God has admitted to much hidden knowledge through deep and blessed experiences, finds
that insensibly his spiritual fervor is depressed. He
cannot go forward in the highest duties of his Christian profession as he once could. Like Elisha, he
needs a minstrel.

3. Another cause of the loss of power is neglect of scriptural doctrine. Much has been said from many standpoints in discussing the beliefs of men. For the present I need but a single point, that a man's conduct is determined by what he believes. If you believe that a man will lie, you will not repose any trust in him. You will not do any business with him where anything has to be trusted to his word. This law, which prevails in the commonest business, holds also when you rise to the plane of a man's religious nature.

What a person believes will determine what he does. If, therefore, one loses confidence in the truths which made him an earnest Christian worker, he will soon cease to be fit for his duties, and like Elisha, will have need of a minstrel.

Now I will not say, as a good many newspapers do, that the *age* has outgrown all old Christian doctrine. I will not say this, because I can't persuade myself that a small circle of men in each city, representing not one-five-hundredth part of the population, and an occasional man in country places, really make the age. I know that circles of so-called free-thinkers arrogate to themselves all the learning there is, and are not just enough to admit that any other men know anything to speak of. I can not admit that any just admeasurement of society will show that these few people are the whole of our age. Other men do know something and think somewhat. The overwhelming

millions deserve to be recognized as something more
than merely a contingent remainder. Nor can I see
that secular editors, who, if true to their business,
must read chiefly the street and other newspapers,
are the best judges of the value of Christian
doctrine.

But every one must admit, that certain currents
can be traced in society, which when they strike
a youthful person of unformed character, will in-
cline him to think that the doctrines his father
believed are unsuited to our time. Then no matter
what blessed experiences he may have had of the
inner life of faith and prayer, as he gives up one
doctrine after another he will feel a growing unfit-
ness for real spiritual work for God. He will need
a minstrel.

I stand upon the principle that for safety and
for real usefulness in life, it is much better to
believe too much than too little. Allow me a very
simple illustration : A few weeks ago I filled an
engagement in the eastern townships. I saluted in
the distance the royal form of grand old Mount
Orford, passed under the shadow of Shefford mountain, and slept where wide Yamaska allowed no
western wind to blow, and saw Owl's Head dark
against the blue clear sky. As a gentleman drove me
from the station to his home, I noticed that the
shafts of his vehicle had a double fastening to the
axle, not only the usual bolt, but a leather strap
also. He told me that among the hills every pre-

caution was necessary to guard against accident. If the bolt slipped, the strap would hold until the vehicle could be stopped and danger averted. And I learned that often even a third protection was used, a chain from the doubletree to the axle of the waggon. Now, my drive of six miles and return was made in perfect safety, and with most pleasant memories I left that smiling home hidden among the hills. In my experience none of the extra precautions were needed.

Last Tuesday afternoon I started on an engagement in a different direction into the level country beyond Laprairie, to the south and west. There was a stage ride of sixteen miles after six in the evening, and it was intensely dark. Our progress was slow, and about ten o'clock the driver began to cry out frantically to his team to stop. The waggon dashed to one side, and before we could realize what was wrong, the wheels on one side were in a ditch two feet deep, and the waggon with its living freight turned fairly over among the small trees. Fortunately no one was injured. We crawled out in the darkness and in the mud and rain, all enquiring what was wrong, and all agreeing that a wheel had come off. But when at last we got a light, it was found that nothing was wrong, but simply one of the bolts fastening the pole to the axle had escaped and caused all the mischief and endangered six lives! Now, a little strap like that I saw among the hills would have prevented all the trouble. It would

have kept the waggon straight in the road until it
could have been stopped. But then in that level
country, why take any precautions ?

Here is to my mind a true view of the value of
doctrine to a religious life. It is better to have
precautions not needed than to fall into danger
for want of them. It is better to believe too much
than too little. A person begins a Christian life in
membership with the church, private prayer, attending prayer-meetings and meetings for religious
fellowships. He feels that he is walking a moun-
tainous road full of dangers, and needs all precautions like the driver among the hills out in the
townships. He is taken by one of the currents I
spoke of. He gets rid of the doctrine of eternal
punishment.

Mount Orford is removed from his world. In its
place is a plain. Atonement in blood is dismissed
from among the doctrines he believes. Yamaska is
now sunk to a plain. He dilutes the inspiration of
the Scriptures until all authority is gone from the
books. Now Mount Shefford has disappeared, and
so pretty soon he is in a great plain like that at
Laprairie and beyond where I was last week, where
no precautions are necessary because there are no
hills. With the doctrines removed out of his faith
his conduct changes. He needs no prayer-meeting,
no Christian fellowship now. He thinks he hears
some rationalizing preacher say that great minds are
living in an atmosphere of prayer, as long as they

desire to know more of God and His will, and (it is rather flattering to him to do so), he believes it, and then neither his evening lamp nor the morning sun ever sees him on his knees any more. He becomes æsthetic, he goes to church twice on Sunday, and that is his religion. He has thinned out his doctrines, taken off his precautions and diluted his practice. He is not in a condition for the highest Christian work. He needs a minstrel.

When last Tuesday there was only one bolt to our carriage, it failed and we went into the ditch in the dark night. When a man has removed faith in scriptural doctrines out of his heart, there is just one bolt that holds him from danger, that is the uncertain life of his body. When that gives away, as with our carriage, he will go into a ditch in the darkness. I know not how deep it may be, but I know it is what the Bible calls hell !

II. The first thing necessary to regain this lost power is the believing and prayerful study of God's Word. There is nothing in the world that so separates a man from the mass and stamps him with his own true individuality. Here we see Noah and Jesus each in his own time standing against the whole world ; Moses and Elijah and Daniel at different periods standing alone, with the king and the whole nation against their single-handed power ; but God, the Lord, was with them. We see Paul undismayed by the contempt of all the learning of Athens. And then its form of address is calculated

to make a man feel that he has a separate responsibility of his own complete in itself. "To him therefore that knoweth to do good, and doeth it not,
to him it is sin."—(Jas. iv. 17.) There is nothing
general here. There is no letting a man down
from his high standard because others do not live
up to that standard. Daniel in Babylon might
say, "All around me regard the king as supreme,
I alone pray to the true God. Why should I not
be content to be as good as others are!" But
if Daniel does say that, he falls and God is no
longer with him. But if Daniel is faithful against
a world, even lions' mouths shall be kept from him.

And so the teaching of all the Bible causes one to
feel that his sin is his own and no one's else. And
so is his virtue. If he builds up truth, purity and
love in his heart, it is something wholly his own.
No one can ever take it from him. Now, this teaching will save a man from being borne down by the
influence and example of others.

Another needful thing is a regular habit of
secret devotion. The hand of the Lord does come
upon men when they are alone with God in prayer.
It was so with Elijah on Carmel ; with Hezekiah
in his sickness ; with Daniel when in danger ; and
with the great and good of all ages, churches and
nations. We often hear a plausible statement that
prayer is elevation of soul and communion with
God, and not external forms. But it is and always
has been a fact, that those souls most effectually

retain their elevation and communion with God, who most regularly observe the outward forms of religion, that is, of course, if they do it understandingly. A condition of spiritual deadness is more likely to disappear when a person habitually devotes himself to secret interviews with God, than if he trusts to chances to find amid social and business duties spare moments for reflection. The grandest pictures have a frame. The picture is worth a thousand dollars, the frame only a few dollars; and yet no artist would exhibit a picture without a frame. So it is with the forms of religion. They are worth little compared to the true and fervent spirit, yet they are necessary to that spirit. And our souls will become empty, withered and dead if we neglect them.

3

QUESTIONING GOD'S GOODNESS.

"It shall come to pass at that time, that I will search Jerusalem with candles, and punish the men that are settled on their lees ; that say in their heart, The Lord will not do good, neither will He do evil."—ZEPH. i. 12.

THIS language describes a certain class of scientific men—the Pantheists—who thoroughly believe that nature is subject to a reign of law, but do not believe much of anything else. They are willing enough to admit that there is a God, if you will admit that He never interferes with the world He has made. Such persons certainly say that the Lord does not do good, neither does He do evil. I have no further mention to make of these teachers.

I am thinking of another class which these words describe. They are persons who have lost their interest in religion, and have no expectation that any good will come from it, while at the same time they do not fear that it will do any harm. They have sunk into a condition of indifference concerning it.

But it is not an uncommon thing for a young man to be in this condition in relation to religion, while he is thoroughly alive and in sympathy with his times in everything else. At any period of life a man may settle upon the lees, so far as religion is concerned, by simple neglect. He abandons prayer, he forgets the Bible, he sets no guard over his sympathies, and pays no attention to the direction in which they run, he is intimately associated with irreligious men, in business, and in social life, while because of their position, he esteems the words of these men at more than their true merit; and so he is gradually led to drop out of one path of Christian effort after another, and the final result is a young man on the lees. He expects nothing from religion, and has lost all enthusiasm for its success.

The language used to describe their state is equally suggestive. They are men " settled on their lees." Now we know that the heavier parts, the earthly particles in any liquid, settle to the bottom, and are called lees. In the margin it is rendered " curdled, or thickened." Some fluids, after standing for a time, curdle, or become thick, and after that do not move easily, or readily fall into the shape of any new dish into which they are put.

The evil and danger of such a condition is that all enthusiasm, all expectation, has gone out of their lives. They are heavy themselves, and unconsciously they come to feel in their hearts that God also is asleep. They think that He will not do good, neither will He do evil.

All the charm of living is lost to a true man when he has no longer any expectation, when he ceases to see God moving everywhere, and to look out for some evidence every hour that His hand is moving great currents all up and down society, and thrashing the nations into the mould of His own thought.

When a person, either old or young, finds himself losing interest in the life of his time, he may be assured that the cause is in himself. It may be due to the weight of years, or to a premature decay of his faculties, because he has worked too hard, or has let his life flow out too fast in pleasure. Mental idleness will produce the same result. Every one knows that men change with age. Any observer of human nature has noticed that with passing years men grow conservative in all their habits of thought. Even politics is not an exception to this rule, if we are to believe the histories of former times.

This growing conservatism is not because things have so improved as to approximate perfection since these same men were young; for the tendency is noticed to have been just the same in men when there was every evidence that things were becoming worse all the time. The change is in the man himself. It is simply a growing dislike of the effort and exertion necessary to adapt one's self to new and changed circumstances, just as in the case of a thickened liquor. This is a natural effect, from the process of growing old. An aged person is raised high above all blame or ridicule on account of his satisfaction with things just as they are. This con-

dition will come to all soon or late ; the only thing to
be thought of is to keep this time of thickening as
far in the distance as possible. It should not be
allowed to force itself upon us sooner than needs be;
we should not welcome it in at the door, or run out
into the street to meet it. Scarcely anything is
more melancholy and depressing than a young man
about sixty years of age, who was born, say thirty-
five or forty years ago, and who thinks that everything as it was a century since was better than it is
to-day. I remember a man of this kind who
preached in my pulpit once, and in the sermon,
among other echoes from the graveyard, he referred
to "that thing which is called love now-a-days."
When we were walking from the church, I recovered
from my sadness sufficiently to ask him what evidence he had of any great change in the quality of
that precious article called love, since he and I made
fools of ourselves on account of it ? By what plea
could he at forty years of age, justify himself for
going around bewailing the degeneracy of the
times ? He ought to wait at least a few years.
People in such a condition, whether old or young,
want religion to be both very respectable and very
respectful. It should respect a man's worldly position, and arrange things pretty lively for low
people, but should discriminate in favor of those
who have thrashed the world into a recognition of
their importance. It should never intrude into private affairs, so as to invade that region in which the

conscience is supposed to dwell. Such people never
want to see or hear anything different from the
usual monotony to which they are accustomed.
Let no awakening or disturbing element have any
place.

Any approach to a revival disturbs them greatly.
Under such circumstances they must lift themselves,
and fight in the best sense, or else run in the worst;
and the idea of having to move around, and possibly to shout, and then to stand rubbing their fast-
stiffening joints and muscles, after having been surprised into an unusual lively movement, seems a
grave contradiction to all proprieties. The consequence is that these curdled people see nothing in an
effort to arouse the world to a sense of its danger
and need but extravagance, and therefore they favor
it with their sweeping condemnation. There may
be conversions that lead thieves to return plunder
to the owners, offering not only contrition but restitution, and that may turn husbands, formerly
drunken, homeward to lonely and heart-hungry
wives, with bread in their hands and peace in their
hearts: but all these good fruits are lost sight of in
the general discomfort caused by a gracious work of
revival. Thickened men settled on the lees cannot
abide such things. Then to be called out to earnest,
personal effort, by motives which they either must
obey or feel intensely uncomfortable, is too much
altogether. To turn aside from their hard-beaten
path to speak a warning to the erring, to win a soul

from its sin, to tell the way of peace through faith in Jesus Christ to the lost wanderer, that one step is the grasshopper which is beginning to be a burden.

To such a state of mind, any change in the service to make it more helpful to some classes of minds, so that it may better lead a refined taste, or encourage a diffident spirit to greater confidence, or impart more strength to the weak and the simple, is an inadmissible irregularity. Any attempt after better methods will require so much lifting of the feet, and shifting of the chair, and getting around in general, before one will know just where he is, that the man who is on the lees will see insurmountable obstacles in the way of every new work.

One good thing may be said about men in this condition—they do not renounce their faith, they are sure to be orthodox, and their high morality is almost as good as assured for a life-time. They so dread exertion that they will not put forth the effort necessary to any great act of immorality. They would hardly spend the breath necessary to swear, if an entirely new order of things should be forced upon the community.

Now this degeneracy of unsympathetic inaction is one of the natural tendencies of our nature, against which we should be on our guard. How to avoid it is worthy of much thought and effort.

1. One remedy is to remember that God has never yet allowed the world to stand still. We turn our

faces toward the past, with our hand to our ear,
that we may catch the echoes that come up from
those weary days of darkness ; but we hear not the
onward movement, as we may hear the startling
thunder, like armed chariots moving forth to war.
We listen to the present, but in the crowding,
trampling multitudes, we hear nothing that is a
positive assurance of progress. Nor can we see in
the rushing myriads any line of orderly movement
onward. No eye can see the moral progress of the
race to better things, as we may see the darkening
cloud climbing up over the face of the sky. Looking
out upon the struggles and conflicts of men, all seems
confusion. No one point can be discerned in the
disorder, where the greatest spirits are cutting
through the darkness a path for all mankind and
drawing them after. But when the long day of
battle is over we can see which army has gained the
field. So we may take our stand at the beginning
of some great epoch of history, and watch the slow
procession of the years toward the next great epoch.
Now we can see the hand of God everywhere. It
has done marvellous things, using every kind of
agency for the advancement of His wise purposes.
Now we see whole centuries given up to war and
destruction. The blood of uncounted hundreds of
thousands has been poured into the earth. The
tenderest affections have been blighted. The rich
and prosperous have been hurled down to poverty
and misery, in the midst of great national con-

vulsions. Whole peoples have been led into slavery. Fair lands have been desolated. Wide territories have been depopulated by famine and pestilence. Yet in some way or other, which the actors never intended nor understood, through all these convulsions the race has been led to something better than was ever before known. After every storm the standard of human progress has been planted a little farther in advance. Men have found themselves in the enjoyment of some new good. The movement of mankind through blood and tears, through graves and sacrifices, has been onward and upward. The light increases. The race has fought its way up from midnight to dawn, and now the noontide is fast hurrying on to meet the children of to-day.

What has done it? Not the genius of conquest, nor that of discovery, for these actors never planned, nor even knew that they were the leaders of the human family up nearer to its goal. It is God alone who has been in all movements of men, causing the evil to spend its force in ways as little destructive as possible, and bending the good towards the highest ends. God alone could see any order or design in the history of nations. As God has been working among our kindred in all ages, we may make sure that He is equally potent in every field of action in our time. We cannot understand why things turn as they do. We seem to be accomplishing nothing. But place your hand over your eyes, and turn your face toward the dazzling future, and

you will see the peoples of the coming time looking
back to our era as the womb of their grand civilization, thanking us for what we now suffer in their
behalf, and wondering how we could endure to live
in such days as these.

2. We need also to remember that God has always
used His Church as a mighty factor in the world's
progress.

There have been times when its character was
such that we of to-day cannot understand how it
could bear the name of the Church at all. It was
low in its aims. It was grovelling in its methods.
It was vile in its morality. Yet even then it was
the best thing that those weary ages preserved to
the world. Take out what it knew, and what it
taught, and what it did, and all the rest that was
in the world might be buried in oblivion, and mankind would be no poorer.

So to-day the Church of Christ is the very best
thing that belongs to this world. The inspiring
Spirit is higher than the written word. The word
is higher than the pulpit that preaches it. The
pulpit is higher than people in the church who
stand around it. Its teaching, notwithstanding
many perversions of truth, is far in advance of the
world's moral practice. The people in the Church
are immeasurably in advance of the masses who
live out of the Church, shaking'off its restraints, and
scorning its teachings. Through His Church the
Almighty God is to-day calling the earth to a better
type of life, and a higher plane of happiness.

3. We should also remember that in the past God has pushed old effects and useless agencies out of the way, and has brought better and more active instruments upon the field.

Some men and some institutions are in the position of advantage for action. They stand next to the tree of success, and more easily and naturally than others can pluck its fruit. They are like the seventh figure to the left in a row of figures. They represent millions, while others stand only for hundreds, or even tens, or perhaps merely units. The Christian Church and the prominent men in it have in every age been in this position of advantage to act upon the world. They are so placed to-day. They can do more than other men equally well equipped in all other respects.

But mark, it is the Church that God uses. It is the truth it holds in possession, the gift of the Spirit which rests upon it; the peculiarly well adapted organization for action which it possesses : this is what He prizes, not the particular men who are in it at any given time. It follows that if those who are providentially so well situated for all action are at any time settled on the lees, and dread any change and effort, and will not move, the event is never prevented, though it may be delayed, by that fact. God will cause such a noise to come tumbling about their astonished heads, that they will either get out of the way, or get up and strike. If they cannot arouse themselves so as to be equal to the claims of duty,

or the demands of the hour, He will leave them at
their ease, but at the same time, without waiting for
them either to get ready for it, or to die, He will
find some one for the occasion—some one not tied up
by traditions or prejudices, who will move, and that,
too, like the lightning around an acute angle. In the
sixteenth century, the noise was Luther's voice. In
the seventeenth, it was Puritanism. In the eighteenth,
He drew John Wesley out of the window of a burning building. In our own time He has sent to grave
men in classical Edinburgh, and in wealthy London,
a Moody and a Booth with their fervency and love
for the souls of men, if by any means whatever they
may be saved.

In the sixteenth century the Church of Rome was
orderly enough, and very respectable, so that it
frowned upon such an irregular thing as Protestantism. It felt strong enough to despise, and trample
into the earth, any such unauthorized movement.
Yet Protestantism lives to-day. And so, a hundred
years later, the starched dignitaries of a dominant
ecclesiastical system stood blazing in the flattering
light around the throne. They tried to crush Puritanism under their indignant feet, but in vain.

And so, too, the Church of Wesley's day was
equally unfit to do His great work for humanity.
It had let the population of the kingdom entirely
outgrow the accommodation of the churches, while,
with becoming dignity, it read its classical service to
those who would hear, and it had neither sympathy

nor interest in any one else. It straightened itself up in shocked amazement when a man was found to seek the welfare of the house of Israel, and stood confounded at Wesley's strange doctrine and irregular methods. Why, he would preach in the streets! It was dreadful! So they cast him out.

Now these men in each case were in the providential place for action, but actually they were worthy successors of the Pharisees who in their pride cast out Jesus as a vain pretender. They scorned and cursed Him, then they condemned and crucified Him; and yet Jesus lives, and He is here to-day.

It is an old truth that God waits no man's convenience. In the affairs of nations it is as it is in the Church. Men who will not or can not move, must get out of the way. Every Charles I. has his Cromwell. Every George III. has his Washington. Every Philip II. has his William the Silent.

This is the law of human progress, both in and out of the Church. God will not wait until those who ought to be His agents are ready. If they are not ready when His time comes, they must give place to others. We must either fill our place or be cast out of it.

Does the thought occur to any mind, whom is this all designed to strike?

1. I answer first of all, it is aimed at myself. I confess that I feel the rush of the world's life around me so intensely that at times it seems diffi-

cult to keep up with it. The heart, wearied with
its fast throbbing, sometimes cries out for a little
rest. But I doubt not that others are in the same
condition. I simply mean to warn against a common danger.

2. My second thought in presenting these warn-
ings is that this church ought to be in a state of
constant revival. It will either be very dead, or
tremendously alive. All its sympathy should be
invoked in the interest of a religion that saves
men's souls. I want to speak words that will help
to remove every possible hindrance out of the way
of a revival that may result in the saving of men. I
would, if I could, strike a blow that would awaken
every man out of a condition of indifference and
hopelessness concerning the church's work.

3. I especially mean my words to be an earnest
call to every one to arouse himself, and stand in
readiness for work. The success of a church, almost
more than anything else, depends upon each person
in it doing something. I have read an incident
that occurred in a thunder-storm. A family in
great alarm had gathered themselves into the middle
of the largest room in the house. The youngest
child suddenly disappeared from the cowering company, and went into one of the dark corners of the
room, and knelt down in prayer. After a few
moments she returned, and glowing with hopefulness,
said, " Well, I have done what I could, anyway."
And what she could do was much. So should every

one connected with a Christian church be able to say
with reference to its great enterprises.

4. There is always danger of overlooking the importance of conversion and sanctification, in other
forms of effort ever rushing upon us. Generally a
church gets what it labors for. If it is for great congregations who come and go as to any fashionable
resort, they can have it if they will pay the price.
If they will have saving power they may have that
also. When God converted Augustine, who dreamed
of what He was going to do with that man? So
even now there may be some one here whom God is
going to use in a similar remarkable work, after
converting him to-night.

5. Last of all, I ask your sympathy with the
Christian Church. Work with it. Sympathize with
its mission. Cherish hopeful feelings concerning its
future. Depend upon it the Church is going to be
in at the final triumph of God and righteousness.
It will be present when truth receives its grand
coronation.

Who would not share its mighty triumph then?
Therefore share its work and lot now, and cultivate
enthusiasm, in looking out upon its future prospects.

GOD'S AGENCY IN EVIL.

" It shall come to pass at that time, that I will search Jerusalem
with candles, and punish the men that are settled on their lees,
that say in their heart, The Lord will not do good, neither will
he do evil."—ZEPHANIAH i. 12.

A WEEK ago I endeavored to show that God does
do good. The whole trend of human events,
under His guiding hand, points to good. The earth is
steadily moving toward a better day.

But the text urges us to enquire if He also does
evil. It is as clearly implied here that He does the
one as the other.

It is important, to begin with, to understand what
is meant by evil. The idea which the word conveys
to our minds is that which causes pain, or distress,
or disappointment, or which interferes with human
happiness. We also generally associate with it
some malignity or delight in others' miseries, on the
part of the one who causes them.

Now with that idea of evil in our minds, we may
well pause before we accept as truth, the statement
that God does evil. His character, as given to us in
the Bible, is goodness ; and ever delighting in good-

ness, happiness and peace. To a being with such a nature all moral evil is impossible. All malice, or hatred, or envy, is eternally excluded from every thought of His heart. We cannot think of Him as delighting in the misery of any creature.

What then remains? In what sense may we think of God as doing evil?

There are two lines along which this text may be interpreted.

I. There is the evil which God does as a discipline. I mean those present evils which are designed for discipline and correction, and through which the offender becomes a nobler creature.

II. Then there is punishment that is retributive. God does this kind of evil by simply allowing it to fall upon men as a natural consequence of their indiscretions and sins.

I. Let us consider first the evil which God uses as a corrective agency. By that is meant some dispensation which causes present distress, or loss, or disappointment, though in the end it will result in happiness. The good, the happiness, which comes out of it is great, out of all proportion to the pain which was suffered. It can only be called evil in the same sense in which the punishment which a loving parent inflicts upon a disobedient child is called evil. But that present punishment may save the child from years, yea, it may be, from infinite ages of suffering. So also may the evil which God uses for purposes of correction. If we speak with

4

strict philosophical correctness, we will not call it evil at all, but good.

In this class we should doubtless count most of the disappointments in our plan in life, and the losses we have to bear, and the failures in reaching what our efforts aim at. Perhaps we should also include here the sickness we suffer; but I have serious doubts if God does use sickness, certainly not often, to correct us for sin.

Now, when by God's direction any of these things fall upon us, it is that they may bend and grind us into better shape, and that they may prune and train us into more refined and exquisite forms of beauty.

Here then is one sense in which we may understand the truth implied in the text.

II. Leaving these forms of evil, if we call them such, we have to consider the evil that comes upon men as a retributive punishment. The word is used for pain or misery that does not result in good. There is a misery that pierces, and pinches, and grinds, and bleeds, and groans through unlimited years, that sweeps onward like a great river wearing its channel deeper and wider as it flows steadily on to the end, or it may be for aye.

Now, does God plan such evil as this? Does He invent it? Does He work it out in His thought and cause it to drop down upon men like thunder from an unclouded sky? That could not even be thought of by anything less than a monster. I remember

in an old sermon once, the language, " God delights
in human groans ; tears and blood are welcome to
His eye." That thought was got from the spirit of
that age, but not from the Bible. It is only in the
freest use of figurative language that God can be
said to do evil so rank as this. He permits it to
come, and the one who allows is sometimes said to
do the deed.

But, even so, we need to proceed with the greatest
caution to an understanding of the way in which
God permits this evil. It is not as we may think
of a man permitting his child to leap into a catar-
act to his certain destruction. He could prevent it
by a touch of his hand, or even by a word, but he
does not. We cannot imagine such a thing as possible. But not so does God permit remediless calamity to fall upon men. I think it was in 1877
that one of the most calamitous railway accidents
of modern times occurred at Ashtabula, Ohio. A
full passenger train went through a bridge. An
Ohio farmer and his wife sat in that train. The
roar of the train prevented their hearing the crack-
ing of the timbers of the bridge. But they felt the
first shock indicating that something was wrong.
The car seemed to leap up. They thought that the
train was simply off the track. Then it seemed to
be going up a steep hill. No doubt the rear end of
the car where they sat sank down first. When it
struck the ice the car was crushed to pieces, and the
man was pinned fast between the side of the car

and a seat. The wife was free. The water was
fast rising at the lower end, and the fire rapidly
approaching them from above. She did all she
could to release her husband. He told her to try to
bend his leg around the seat, and, if possible, to
break it. He thought if it were broken, he would
be relieved from his cramped position, and might
extricate himself. Her efforts to do this were in vain.
The fire was fast approaching ; now it seized upon
her garments. She had formed a plan in her mind,
and when the fire came she began to lay cushions of
car seats upon her husband, intending to sit upon
them in the hope that while she was being consumed,
some providential relief might save him. This, however, he would not allow her to do. He compelled
her to leave the burning wreck, and she went out,
her clothing in flames.

Now the manner in which that woman permitted
her husband to perish, is somewhat as God allows
remediless evil to fall upon men. She did all in her
power to save him before she abandoned him to his
fate. The calamity was not designed or planned by
her. He chose to make the journey, well knowing
that trains were sometimes wrecked. Death came
to him in the regular course of unavoidable events.

So it is with God's government. He has appointed
and ordained the system of things which prevails
throughout the universe. This system is calculated
to bring the greatest possible amount of happiness
to God, and all His creatures, throughout all the ages ;

still, it is possible that under it evil, from which there is no escape, may spring into existence. This arises from the unalterable and irreconcilable enmity which exists between the serpent and the seed of the woman, between love and hatred, between purity and lust, between honesty and fraud, between truth and falsehood, between a benevolent regard for all mankind, and the bony-fingered cupidity of covetousness, which grasps after all, and tries to monopolize it for self; in short, between all that is right and all that is wrong; so that it is inevitable that sin will be followed by pain and anguish. Nothing but misery can ever spring as the last result from moral baseness.

This is not only true of this world, but of all the wide universe. There is not a spot owned by God anywhere, not a place big enough to hold an intelligent creature of any order, in all the realm over which He reigns, wherein sin will not, before it has run its course, cause a pang to pierce the soul. This is a natural consequence, and it is impossible that this can be otherwise, and the order of the universe be what it is. If the order were changed so as to make anything else possible, it would be changed in such a way as to be less productive of good, or of the happiness of all, than it now is.

If, therefore, men will fully choose alliance with the serpent, if they will wind around their souls, and bury up in their natures the love of what is false and foul, then it must follow that after a few

bright days of sinful pleasure, they will be stung
with the serpent's poison, and ensnared and bound up
with the chains of their own treachery. The evil
impression upon their hearts will become indelible.
If a light be flashed before a glass and then taken
away, it will leave no impression, but if often
repeated it will leave an impression that will abide.
The twig carelessly bent in passing from day to day,
at last has an inclination that is permanent, and continues throughout the life of the tree. So a man's
conscience may become unalterably depraved, and
then he will find a deepest hell begun in himself;
and even if it were possible that prayer might open
any door of escape, this deep-seated love for the foul
atmosphere of curses would prevent any deliverance
through that door. When, then, we say that God
allows these irretrievable evils to fall upon man, it
is only saying that the order of nature, which is
every way for the best, is allowed to take its course,
and to work out its legitimate results. It is something like this. Every railroad must have its
terminus somewhere. Let us suppose that it is a
season in which the yellow fever is raging in New
Orleans. The pure, bracing air of the north is full
of health and life. A man stands in a station at
Chicago. At one platform is a train which will
carry him down the Mississippi to New Orleans. At
another is one waiting which will start in a few
moments for Manitoba. The man knows perfectly
well the different chances for life in the two places.

Yet he wilfully goes aboard the train pointing towards the south, and soon it is thundering away on its
course towards the plague-stricken city. But he need
not stay on board. There are fifty stations, at either
of which he may get down and retrace his steps. But
he finds genial spirits in the car. They eat and
drink, and smoke together, they talk and laugh and
play, and the hours pass rapidly. He never once
thinks of the end, until the train is rushing into the
doomed city. The sharp whistle of the locomotive
reminds the passengers that they have now gone too
far to escape the danger. Already the poisoned air
is rushing in at the window. They look out on
every side upon the ghastly evidences of pain and
death and sorrow. A day or two later it is known
that this man has taken the fever and died.

Now we are going to fix the blame in this case
upon the right parties. Will you reproach the railroad company for bringing this evil upon this man?
Every one says that would be most absurd. What
is the fact? The railway company has established
an order of things by which the welfare of the
country is greatly advanced. But under this order
of things which it has established it was possible
for a man to run into this danger, and to bring
upon himself this evil, which is without a remedy
in this world. By just so much and no more, the
railway company does the evil which the man and
his family suffer in his death.

Now it is in a manner perfectly similar to this,

that God may be said to do the evil which men
suffer in consequence of their sins and follies. The
railroad is a great good to all travellers. and to commerce. It is not possible to prevent a foolish man
from using it to advance the ends of folly. So
God's universe is the most perfect of which it is
possible to conceive. Still men may make such a
use of their privilege in it as to cause the whole
world to fall down upon them.

> " For such God's holy law, in written word,
> In nature writ, that they who willing gird
> Themselves in sin, as in a mantle warm,
> In guilty ignorance their souls deform,
> Shall find in chosen sin their direst curse,
> A heavier load than all the universe ? "

The blow will be sure to fall some time. The sky
will be written over with wrath to the eye of the
guilty. The only way to avoid the curse of sin is
to avoid the sin.

One day I examined a grand edition of Milton's
" Paradise Lost." It was the Doré edition, and
splendidly illuminated with the matchless pictures
from that master's peerless hand. One of these pictures represented Adam and Eve almost immediately
after the fall. They are far enough removed from
their sinful act to begin to realize the terrible con-
sequences of it. The deep blackness of their eclipse
is beginning to flow over their souls. They stand,
dressed in their extemporized garments of fig leaves,
in an attitude that indicates a feeling that everything

good has gone out of their grasp. The light is fast
fading from their eyes. They can now only see the
barrenness of the rocks over which they bend.
With consummate skill the artist has thrown into
their faces all the indefinable anguish of a hell
already begun. Still there is room for the imagination to work around such a picture, and if you will
allow this, you can weep in sympathy with misery
like this, so deep that no language can give it form,
but which wails out upon you in suggestive sym-
bolism.

As I looked upon that picture the thought pressed
upon me with overwhelming power, that picture is
an allegory, representing the bitter, searching, rend-
ing truth that lies buried up in the story of all sin.
They found it an easy way in, but the path once
entered they were already in the hot flames of hell.
So it always is. So it will prove with you, my
beloved friend, if you dare to tempt hell and death
by making the trial. You will find that the way
down will be made very attractive and full of promise. The dalliance with its charms might draw an
angel under its thrall. But after the sleep, adorned
with fantastic visions, comes the terrible awakening
to hard pressing realities. After the thrilling intoxi-
cation of pleasure come the sharp pains of nature's
readjustment. When one is going down into the pit
of guilt he thinks only of pleasure, or gain, to be
realized. After the act is done and the pleasure is
drunk, or the gain is wasted, there comes the bitter

remembrance of much good lost. The sensibility that offered stern and sure resistance to evil is gone. The sweet security of innocence, that, like the dusty covering of the grape, once removed can never be replaced; the door of opportunity, open in all directions, now forever closed; the unquestioning esteem of good men turned into looks of doubt; the sense of the divine favor once streaming down into the heart like guiding sunlight, are now withdrawn, and the soul is left in a darkness that is close and cold and helpless.

Oh, this bitter awakening after a course of sin is inevitable. No man can escape it. He may bury himself in indulgences which induce forgetfulness for a few years, but from his first step downward, the messenger that shall lift the veil of his illusion is moving toward him with hurrying feet. It is the avaricious man, before whom the door of fraud or theft stood so temptingly open, and it was so easy to enter in, and it seemed so safe in there. It is the thoughtless maiden, or the weak wife who, carried away with excitement and drunk and silly with love, thinks that it is romantic and grand to stake everything on love. It is the growing boy, or the young man who dallies and trifles with drink, because no nerve in his body has ever shown a sign of tremulousness, and he foolishly thinks that it will be ever so; or who allows his yet scant stock of wisdom to be borne down by his affluent physical power, and then shouts his reckless, taunting bravado in the face of all virtue, and in pursuit of soft indulgences gains a knowledge which no youth is yet fit to know, and which no young man can venture to know without tempting damnation into his own soul. No matter who it is, or where or when, it will be the experience of Adam and Eve over again. The one fatal step is taken, the deed is done, the poison has begun to flow, and a fathomless depth of woe must be drunk dry before that one sin has run its full course.

A thought, shaded somewhat with doubt, has been growing in some minds as I have gone on. I will try to state it for you.

It is like this. The text represents that God bears the same relation to the doing of the good and to the doing of the evil. Now, the argument in this sermon makes out that God only does evil by allowing it as the natural result of the order of things He has established in nature. Why, then, will it not follow that He does good in the same way? But this is all that the Pantheistic philosopher claims, that the world is under natural laws, and God never interferes with its operations, either for good or ill.

But all this does not follow from the argument. The goodness of God's character will prevent His interfering with the established order of things to do evil; but the very qualities which hinder Him from interfering in this way will prompt Him to interfere to do good.

It now remains to show how He has interfered
for the sake of the human race, or to do good.

1. The first example of this is the gift to the world
of the Lord Jesus Christ. Go and stand by the
cross, and think if you can that God has never interfered with the affairs of this world for the good
of men. The import of the cross is that as long as
a man is alive in this world he has the privilege of
beginning again. That is what forgiveness of sins
means. It does not mean that in all respects a forgiven man is the same as if the sin had never been
committed. That cannot be. In some respects a
man can never be what he would have been if he
had never sinned. If in a brawl, while he is trying
to wound some one else, he receives a gash across the
face, the scar will remain there. Nothing but death
and decomposition will remove it. So, in many
other particulars, forgiveness does not make the
man the same as if he had never sinned. But this
much it does do: it gives every man a chance to
begin his life upon a new plan. A merchant
changes from the retail to the wholesale. I ask,
" Are you giving up your business ? " He answers,
" No ; but I am changing the plan of my business."
So in any calling a man may change his plan and
methods. He cannot change the mistakes he has
made, or perhaps recover the losses sustained
through those mistakes, but he can adopt a plan
which will prevent similar errors in the future.

Now, this is just what Christ has made possible

to every man. He cannot alter the fact of his past sin. It cannot be wholly undone, but the legal penalty of it may be wholly removed. This done, the man may have another chance. He may begin again, and make the best of his chances during the remaining years of his life.

Are there not some here now who remember the mistakes of the past and would like to begin again ? How often men say, " Oh, that I could live my life over again!" That cannot be, but any one may live the remainder of his life better than what has gone before. The past has built its monument for you. It is the impressions that have been made permanent upon your heart for good or evil; some are good, some are bad. During the past seven days some have learned new sacrifices for virtue, and some to commit new sins. Oh, let us here and now lay down the vow to put ourselves from henceforth in the hands of God, to do His will, and serve His holy cause.

2. God also interferes in order to win men from the path that is leading them down to ruin. Every church built is such an interference. Open or closed, on Sabbath or any other day, it is a silent appeal to all who pass it to turn from the evil to the good. So is the dawn of every Sabbath day. Its quiet, its holy restfulness, the well understood nature of its employments, all that pertains to it, is an appeal to men to turn to God.

But more than this God does. He sends His

ministers with His word of appeal, to win and draw
men away from all evil courses. They urge and warn,
and with affectionate persuasions try to win men,
and the Holy Spirit comes to the heart in a thousand
ways of winning entreaty and persuasive influence.
Providence also opens wide doors through which all
who will may flee from the impending danger. A
young man is held down to a sinful course by the
influence of evil companions, but unaccountably the
one who had the greatest control over him is caused
to remove to another part of the country, or even to
another land. It is the hand of Providence opening
before that young man a way of escape from the
sins and sinful associates of his past life.

3. It is not uncommon when the crash of irretrievable ruin falls upon a person for him to complain against God. He asks, "If God is good why did
He allow me to go on thus to my ruin?" I answer,
"You have been running all your life with heedless
speed towards the present hour, and all the time
God has been trying to prevent you. He has sent
you call after call, opportunity after opportunity,
warning after warning. Again and again you have
seen the ruin of others when pursuing the same path.
But with these things before your eyes you would see
no handwriting of God written in black, threatening
characters against the sky; you would see in them
no hand in mercy stretched out to aid you. You
would go on to the bitter end in your way to ruin.
There now remains nothing for you but to live

through the dark, dreary, and cheerless day upon which you have awakened.

4. But he expostulates further, "If God is omnipotent, why did He not prevent me, and compel me to turn?" That is a very foolish question to ask. It means, why did not God make you at first a tree or a stone? The stone is prevented by God from going to ruin, so is a mole and a snail. They are not capable of knowing or feeling any misery. To have made you such a creature, instead of making you a man, would have been the only way in which God could have absolutely prevented you from being lost. Omnipotence cannot do some things because they are inconsistent with physical force. Tell me to remove a mountain with my hands. Give me time enough and I will do it. But if you ask me to drive the light out of a room by beating it with my hands, I have to reply that it is impossible, I cannot accomplish it if you give me an eternity. The two things are not adapted to act upon each other. So omnipotence is equally unadapted to act against the will of a free moral agent. If God saved you from ruin by the exercise of His omnipotence, He must, as the first act of that omnipotence, change you into something different from what you are. In the change you would become a creature to which it would be of no value to be saved. Man is capable of being happy in heaven or miserable in hell, because he is capable of knowing God. If this capacity were taken away it would

be of no value to get into heaven. But while he possesses that capacity he is free to choose or reject.

5. Here, then, we stand. God does evil through the regular course of things being allowed to proceed and to develop their legitimate results. Whether or not the evil befalls you, will depend upon where you stand. If your life is bad; if your view is so filled up with what is near that you can scarcely feel the effect of the distant; if the present presses upon you and fills you so completely that the future is all shut out; if you so live in the pleasures and excitements of the body that you feel but slightly or not at all the influence and claims of the moral and spiritual world; then you are allowing a leverage to be placed under you which will hurl you with infallible precision from your rock of self-confidence down into a fathomless depth of perdition.

But while God is permitting this to go on, He is appealing by all powerful motives, and striving by all reasonable means to lead every one into paths that will end in happiness and peace. Our duty is to keep our hearts open to all moral motives. We are guilty if we allow ourselves to grow dead to His appeals. We should not consent to become indifferent to the gracious offers by which He appeals to us, and tries to help us. If we are willing to receive the good He is willing to do us, we will never feel in our own experience that He does evil.

THE MIND OF CHRIST.

"Let this mind be in you which was also in Christ Jesus."
—PHILIPPIANS ii. 5.

"AS a man thinketh in his heart so is he." So said Solomon, but Jesus also taught the same truth : " Not that which goeth into the mouth, but that which cometh out of the mouth, defileth a a man." "Those things which proceed out of the mouth come forth from the heart." " For out of the heart proceed evil thoughts," etc. " These are the things which defile a man." It is not then what the hand does, or the mouth speaks, but what the heart thinks, that declares what manner of man a person is. I say, " What one's heart thinks," because in the sense in which the word is used here, the mind means the habitual thoughts of a person.

But in what thoughts then ought I to indulge? " Let this mind be in you which was also in Christ Jesus." To have habitually such thoughts as Jesus had is to have attained to the very highest type of manhood. This is true Christianity.

I. True Christianity requires that there be in us the mind which was in Christ in relation to the affairs of this world.

5

He was in, but not of this world. He used it, but
did not love it. It belonged to Him, He did not
belong to it. He never sold Himself to it. He never
allowed it to get Him into its power as some men
do. I think we express the whole truth on this point
when we say that His relations to this world never
led Him into sin. I think that all sin grows out of
our relations to each other or to God.

We are certainly led into most of the sins which
we commit by our thoughts about this world or
the people in it. We cannot therefore say any
better thing of Jesus than that while in this world
His thoughts never led Him into sin.

I will try to state what His mind was in relation
to this world under a few separate heads, as including in His mind, sympathy, unselfishness, and
honesty.

1. In relation to this world Jesus had a sympathetic mind. He left us in one sentence a rule of
life which we may be sure He observed in His own.
We have heard it called the golden rule, Matthew
vii. 12: "Therefore all things whatsoever ye would
that men should do to you, do ye even so to
them."

Now, when we were children, nothing seemed
more simple than to observe that rule of life. But
the wisdom which attends upon riper years discov-
ers that it is really a difficult command to obey perfectly. I am to do to another what I would have
him do to me. But perhaps he will not like what I

like. Maybe what will be good for me will not be good for him. An idle, ragged boy was asked what he would like to do in heaven, and he said he would like to swing on a gate all day long. Now, suppose that in accordance with this rule that boy should get off the gate on which he is swinging some day, and offer to allow his bent old grandfather to get on it and have a swing, it would no doubt be a great act of self-denial on the part of the boy; yet riding the gate would hardly be suitable to the old grandfather. The boy has not hit the mark though he has obeyed the golden rule.

Now this is certainly an extreme case, used by way of illustration. But we are often discovering that we have not reached our aim when we have honestly done to others what we would have them do to us.

I do not speak in this way to start difficulties. I know that we will each discover difficulties enough for himself. But I allude to this difficulty as one of many illustrations of the truth that it requires much common sense, and much sympathy with humanity, as well as a genuine conversion, to live as a Christian is expected to live. No preacher can tell in his sermon, no manual can lay down in rules, the art by which one Christian may make his walk and conversation as beautiful in the eyes of men as some other has made his. This much we may do. We may each become, through Christ, equally acceptable to God, so far as our past sin is concerned.

We may each be forgiven, and so be admitted into the full favor of God, and be full heirs of heaven. With this we must be satisfied, so far as equality is concerned. In the estimate of men the lives of those who are equally sincere will differ from each other as much as their faces, or their intellectual attainments. According to the measure of a man's good sense, and of his sympathy, but not according to his sincerity, or the genuineness of his conversion, will he appear to men to adorn the doctrine of our Lord and Saviour Jesus Christ, which he professes.

Hence it is that I say that Jesus had a sympathetic mind. He entered into people's feelings. He by sympathy with them was able to discern their characters, and to feel their wants. To use an expression that has now become very common, He could put Himself in the place of another, and then, feeling what would be appropriate in the case, He did as He would have them do to Him in similar circumstances. And this is just what this precept means. We should do unto others what we would have them do to us if we were in their condition or circumstances.

Now, no one ever found it so difficult to do this as Jesus did. He was surrounded by people who were ignorant and malicious. It is very hard for refined and intelligent people to have to come into contact with such persons. When we fall in with stupid persons we instinctively want to take them by the

two shoulders, and cause them to vibrate back and
forth, with a speed more agreeable to us than to
them, and which will cause them to regard their
own breath as for a time an unattainable luxury.
We cannot quite understand why men should be
stupid when the sun is shining, and babies live with
their eyes open. When we meet with the malicious we withdraw into ourselves, very much as we
shrink away from a serpent. We want to have
nothing to do with them. We cannot bear the thought
of going with them, and in any sense sharing in their
fortunes or sufferings. As to their sufferings, we
feel very much inclined to say that it serves them
right. Yet Jesus was in the midst of such all His
earthly life, and never spoke unkindly to one of
them. His words never brought pain or calamity
to one of His bitterest foes. We know that He
judged the erring with gentleness. He stooped to
reach the weak. His heart throbbed with helpful
pity for the suffering and the needy and the sick.
He adapted himself with equal ease to the aged and
the young. He entered into the pleasures of social
life. He was present at the marriage in Cana of
Galilee. I have heard it said that He never laughed.
I do not believe it. He would not have been
true either to His own manhood, or to the world into
which He came to live as other men, if He had not
sometimes laughed. We may depend upon it, that
there was no phase of life peculiar either to age or
youth, experienced either by male or female, with

which Jesus did not enter into lively sympathy.
Though He could not himself enjoy many things
that other men enjoyed, still He knew that if He
were in the same circumstances He would enjoy
them. So far as He could do so without sin, He
entered into other people's joys, and did what He
could to make each happy in his own way. But in
working out this plan of life He allowed neither
mirth or sadness to lead Him into sin.

Now let us have the same mind. Let us, in sympathy, go with others as far as is right, even though
we do not find our pleasure in the same way they
are accustomed to do. It is Christ-like in age to
bend to the weakness and silliness of youth. It is
Christ-like in youth to respect, and in a measure to
appreciate and enjoy the egotism, and slowness, and
love of what is buried deep in the past. The idle
boy need not give his place on the gate to his aged
grandfather, but he may listen attentively to the
old man's stories of the days when he was young,
and which in his thought are ever robed in the
golden hues of the setting sun of life's day, and
are more glorious than anything of the present time.
That is what Jesus would have done. Neither of
the extreme conditions of life can enjoy what most
pleases the other, or would seek it from choice, but
to sympathize with each other is to obey the golden
rule. It is to have the mind of Christ in regard to
such things.

But like Him we must watch, and be sure to stop

before sin enters. There is danger in mirth; yet we need not put it away altogether. The pleasures of social life are attended with danger; yet we must mingle in social life. Danger also lurks along the path in which every man must walk in pursuit of his business; still no one may wholly abandon the work of his daily calling. Age and youth have each their dangers; but men must take their chances in them all. The right way is to have the mind of Jesus, with respect to abstaining from all appearance of evil. We must ask ourselves, again and again, concerning many things in our pleasures and amusements, and methods of business, would Jesus have done this? would He have gone there? Now as I start these questions it is not needful that you begin to question what particular things may be in my mind, or what I may imagine you to be habitually doing which I would question the propriety of; but rather let your thoughts fasten upon anything which may occur to you in your own life, and urge these questions concerning this particular thing. I do not know your life so perfectly, that I should suggest to you what things you should bring to the test of the mind of Christ. But you do know your own life; therefore you may with propriety ask yourself concerning one thing and another, would Jesus have done what I do in this case? If I were sure that He would have done it, would I reverence Him as I have always done?

2. Jesus had also *an unselfish mind.* One great

vice of humanity is selfishness. Some want all for
themselves. They are not happy if others have
anything. But some again are quite willing that
others should be happy if they themselves can only
have all they want first. Indeed, they would prefer
that others should be comfortable, once they themselves are satisfied; but they cannot rise into the idea
of sacrificing anything in order that others may
have their desires. And so the world goes on in its
weary way, witnessing a constant struggle after
things that ought to be shared so as to secure the
equal comfort of all. There is nothing but the mind
of Christ that offers any resistance to this clamor
and conflict of universal selfishness. Men only rise
above it and throw it off just in proportion as they
come to have in them the mind of Christ. After
Napoleon's fall, in 1815, the great powers of Europe
met in council to arrange the affairs of the world so
that it might run along for a time in peace. Upon
no part of the earth did they lay their hand so
heavily as upon Italy. You remember that Italy
had in some parts been subject to republican gov-
ernments for ages. Genoa and Venice taught the
principles of free government to the world long
before nations now in the vanguard of civilization
had begun to awaken out of slavery. Well, this
grave council of the nations placed every part of
Italy under an absolute despotism, with one single
small exception. They recognized the little republic of San Marino. It was on the top of a small

mountain standing out of the range of the Apennines, and embraced only a few hundred people. It seemed like a stroke of sarcasm on the part of the powers to leave liberty in the hands of a few hundreds upon a mountain top, looking down upon a black and hopeless night of universal despotism. But that little light shone farther than they knew. Italy had known the meaning of liberty, and could not forget it. It reached up after it, and rested not for nearly seventy years, until at last it had washed away in blood the stains of tyranny from the land. Well, now, that little light of liberty on one small mountain was to Italy what the mind of Christ is in a world of universal selfishness. It shall conquer in the end. It is conquering now. He was always giving, rarely receiving. An apostle quotes His golden words, " It is more blessed to give than to receive." None of the evangelists record this saying, but His whole life endorses it. The sternest words He ever uttered do not contradict it. His severest words relate to man's punishment because of sin. But He never spoke of punishment like a selfish man, to gratify the burning passion of the passing moment. He declared against sin, and doomed it to punishment in such terms of tender regret, that all who were willing to forsake it felt that in Him they would find the helpful love of a true friend. No one else ever so hated sin and so loved the sinner. He died that He might brand sin as forever and irretrievably bad. He gave His life that He might lead the sinner back to God and heaven.

3. Jesus had also *an honest mind.* Now there is abroad a prevalent idea that success is the thing to be attained. That the question is, has a man succeeded? Has he brought anything to pass? If so, he is to be crowned. The world has nothing to do with questions as to the methods by which success is reached. This view is excused by the consideration that the world is gross and ignorant, and does not know what is best for itself. It must be led against its own will, and afterwards it will perceive that it was best that it should be so managed. But this plausible reasoning is gravely at fault. Its chief merit is that it flatters supremely the self-conceit of the few who happen to be at the time at the wires, allowing them to feel that they are in some sense prophets, and that though the world does not know what is best for it, they do. They are so much exalted above the heads of others, you know. Now, this is certainly very pleasant to their mighty dignities, but the world has not many prophets, and it would be much better without some of those who thus constitute themselves prophets for its benefit. The world has been put back two steps where it has been advanced one, by all the deeds that cunning managers have done by tricks and dishonest devices, imagining that the world was too stupid to understand them.

Here, again, the mind of Christ offers the only

protest. Once more the little republic of San
Marino shines out upon the dark absolutism that
dominates all Italy. The mind of Jesus was an
honest mind. He always spoke the exact truth. In
all His dealings with men He stood upright and
even as a great granite wall. He raised both hand
and voice in straightforward and easily understood
condemnation of the falsehood, and shams, and
make believe, and double dealing, and sly frauds,
which the customs of ages had excused and justified
and tried to make honorable, and which custom
still allows. He would rather sleep upon the bare
face of a rock than lie on a bed of down at the price
of deception. What He could not accomplish by
honorable and fair means, He left to be done by
other ages. If He could not lead in the great things
His heart desired, and which He knew to be for the
good of mankind, by proper methods, He compla-
cently allowed their entrance to be indefinitely
delayed. He trusted implicitly in Providence to
bring all things out right in the end, in spite of the
evil devices of men.

Now, in nothing more than in this respect do men
need to have in them the mind of Christ. We ought
to recognize that there are right methods of doing
right which should be scrupulously observed. Let
us come back to pay honor to honesty, truth and
righteousness. If the world's stupidity, ignorance,
or obstinacy will not allow us to do what we see
plainly will be best for mankind in the end, then let

the world wait for a while. It is pretty well used
to waiting for the good it has received in the past.
It is not necessary that we compel it to receive all
that our conceit points out to us to be best for it.
Other wise and good men will live and act long after
we have gone down into silence. The fact of
achieving a success is not now, nor ever was, a sufficient atonement for using dishonest methods in
reaching our success. Let us learn, like Christ, to
do right, and then leave the world in the hands of a
wise, superintending Providence to work all things
out as they should be in the end.

II. Let us have the mind of Christ in respect to the
visible Church and outward religion. He did not
find a perfect Church in the world by any means. It
was as bad as anything that has appeared at any
subsequent time. Its walls were broken down, and
it was open on every side to the strokes of the critical believer, and the sharp thrusts of the scoffing
infidel. There were the depraved customs which it
had inherited from preceding ages, the absurd traditions it had engrafted upon the Word of God, clothing them with an authority equal to inspiration
itself, the wicked superstitions which had grown
rank with long indulgence, the utter rottenness of
the lives of its chosen and distinguished leaders, the
multiplication of sects within it and their bitter
antagonism to each other. In all these respects it
had sunk as low, and in some respects lower, than
the Church weighted by similar abuses in any subse-

quent period of time. There was many a gross deformity calling for the hammer of the image-breaker, or for the torch of the purifying flame, or for the pruning knife of the ruthless reformer.

Yet bad as that Church was, Jesus did not despise it. He recognized it in His work and attended its services, and held fellowship with its members. He cared not for the church organization, but He did care for humanity, and He saw in the Church the most efficient agency with which to reach the world. Hence, He became not a railing accuser without, but a respectful reformer within.

Let this mind be in you. The Church has never been perfectly pure. There has yet been no time when vileness might not hide its head within its sanctuary. On this account men have assumed various attitudes toward it. Some withhold themselves from it altogether. They pretend—yea, they say—that they live better out of the church, than its members do in it. It is as though some clerk of the Allan Steamship Company had not been accommodating to a passenger about a berth, and henceforth he should determine never again to cross the ocean in a steamer. He will go on a piece of bark. He will purchase a canoe.

Yet others renounce the Church with an affectation of excellence and piety that reveals a magnificent conceit, and which assumes that they embody in themselves a purer and better Church than the Church that through the ages has borne a steadfast

witness for the truth. Their piety is marked by an
almost hatred of any who do not accept their ideas.
They grow more sectarian than any Church of any
age in the past.

Now these methods of treating the Church are both
weak and irreligious. A child ought to see that a
Church can be no better than its individual members.
A thoroughly bad man may work his way in among
others who are perfectly sincere, and as pure as men
may be in this world. Every devout person who
comes into the Church makes it better. By just so
much as each will do his utmost to make the Church
better and purer by making his own life so, will the
Church become what all true men within it desire
that it shall be.

III. Yet again, let us have the mind of Christ in
relation to God and heaven.

We may safely say that in knowing Jesus, we
know one who never turned His eyes toward the sky
with any mists of doubt in them as to the existence
of God, or toward the future shaded with any cloud
of uncertainty. Now, here is one of the weak
points in connection with our religious life. We
would be more certain of the existence of God. The
old cry of the disciples again and again breaks forth
into language, "Lord, show us the Father, and it
sufficeth us." Who would not desire to see his own
father? We are taught to believe that He is, but
we never saw His face. It seems almost too much
for faith to go on for a whole lifetime without any

assurance as to His existence. It is true He was seen
by Moses, face to face ; but that was very long ago,
and the world is now weary with waiting. Why
does He not humor our weakness, and come out
sometimes from behind His impenetrable veil ? Why
does He not at least reach out a visible hand that
we may grasp, or feel its touch, or at least see it
plainly ? These questions arise in our minds in our
weaker moments. We do not admit that they are
doubts, much less that they are sceptical ; but they
come upon us again and again. Then they are
strengthened by the assaults of some who have
grown into open unbelievers. These break out in
strong and bold assertion, denying that there is any
God. We do not believe them, but their violence
adds fuel to the rising flame of our doubts and
questionings. Thus in spite of ourselves, the
thought will arise, " What if there is no God ? " and
close upon its track follows another, " What if
there be no future life ? " What if all the races of
men who have trampled upon each other as they
have hurried across this scene of action have disappeared upon the other side, and will never appear
again ? What if all the great and mighty men of
the past in thought and action, are not now anywhere in existence, and have gone out of all conscious interest and activity in the universe ? Our
thoughts will interest themselves in these questions
in spite of us. Most men find in the circumstances
of this world enough to make them willing to

remain here forever, under favorable conditions, but
all know that this is impossible ; hence the activity
of thought about the future. If we might but
pass through death but for a single moment, and
then return, how much better we could perform our
task here! How much better men we would be
with the assurance thus given !

Well, now, there is some help in knowing that one
who was as truly a man as we are passed through
the same life as ours, and never once felt a doubt
upon any of these intensely interesting points.
When He spoke of his own origin it was with the
utmost certainty. "The Father which sent me."
"I am come from the Father." There was no confusion in His mind as to how He came into existence. He had not to decide whether God made
Him, or a confluence of molecules chanced to throw
Him upon the surface just as He was.

Then He never seemed to think of the Father as
far removed. He spoke of Him as always intimately near. "I will pray the Father." God was
near, so as to be easily addressed. God was for His
help and benefit. Think of it. A man to whose
mind never came the thought, "What if there is no
God!" Who never stood by His dead with any doubt
if He should ever meet them again. He knew that
the "Father raiseth the dead and quickeneth them."
And He was always just as certain about His
own future. "I ascend unto my Father and your
Father, and to my God and your God."

We cannot but feel that our little being is immeasurably exalted and adorned by relationship with such a man, one who while in this life felt that He belonged as much to the unseen world as to the seen, that the future life was as real to Him as the present.

Let this mind be in you. But you say, here is my difficulty. How can I be as confident as He was? Had He not been with the Father before the world was? I have nothing but my faith. If I also had seen the Father as He had, I would never doubt. Now it is just here that we are aided by the mind of Jesus. We know that He had been with the Father. We have the historical fact of His resurrection ever with us. I am as sure that Jesus rose from the dead as I am that I exist. I am just as sure that that man whom I call Christ had actually seen God, that He died and rose again, as I am of any facts. Because I am sure of this, it is not necessary that I also see the Father. If I steadfastly believe that He was actually with the Father, then it is as well as if I also had seen Him. Is there no comfort in these reflections, in the times of our sorrow? You sit by your flower-strewn graves, and you long for some token that will be an assurance to you that your dead still exist, and yet feel some interest in you. You would be satisfied with very little, the falling of a shadow as from a white, sunlit wing, a whisper low and sweet, not so much heard as felt, a dream full of fond remem-

6

brance, and of tender interest—anything whereby
you might know that they yet exist. But no signal
is raised from the distant shore of that waveless
sea, not even an echo comes back to you in answer
to your call. You have the thought that so small a
thing would be granted to you if there were any
future life.

But here again and always Jesus is our help. He
has been through the gates of death, and has returned and shown Himself to men. He hath by
His resurrection " brought life and immortality to
light." If we know Him, by grasping His hand we
grasp the hands of all our dead. In His voice we
recognize the voices of all the saints who have
passed on before, and are now standing upon the
shining shore. To know Him is as good as if we
knew again, or saw again all of our kindred who
have passed away. Let this mind be in you.

IV. We may spend a word upon the question, how
can we come to have this mind of Christ ?

1. The first thing required is that we be regener-
ated in our natures. The Divine Spirit alone can
put us in the way of attaining such excellence.
No work of character-building can put us in the
way of this great good. The renewing of the Holy
Ghost must give us the inspiration.

2. We must study the words and works of Jesus.
When an actor would present one of the plays of
Shakespeare on the stage, he chooses the character
he designs to personate, and then reads the play and

all the history of the times, and everything else
bearing on the period that will help him to fully
enter into the character of the person whom he has
chosen to personate. So do with Christ, and thus
enter into His mind.

3. Love Him. Love creates likeness. The man
who has lived with the wife of his youth in perfect harmony finds a growing likeness between himself and her. Others mark the resemblance. It is
not confined to speech alone, but extends to the expression of the countenance, the gestures, and gait,
and the form of the thoughts. So will love to
Christ greatly advance the likeness to His thought.

IN CHRIST JESUS.

" Therefore if any man be in Christ he is a new creature ; old things are passed away ; behold all things are become new."— 2 Cor. v. 17.

OUR study is the significance of the words " in Christ." The expression is common with Paul: " I knew a man in Christ;" " There is therefore now no condemnation to them that are in Christ." His writings all indicate an exceedingly intimate union between the Christian and Christ— the saint and the Saviour. To know what it is to " be in Christ " is to understand perfectly this intimate union.

1. Many ideas come up in illustration of the relation, and we take first the derivation of life from Christ.

To be in Christ is to derive life from Him. Many passages contain this truth, as Gal. ii. 20 : " I am crucified with Christ, nevertheless I live, yet not I, but Christ liveth in me." And also Col. iii. 3 : " Ye are dead and your life is hid with Christ in God." And again, Phil. i. 21 : " For me to live is Christ." But there is one passage in which this truth is set forth in the most striking manner. It is in Chapter xv. of the Gospel by John: " I am the true vine." "I am the vine, ye are the branches." "Abide in Me and I in you. As the branch cannot bear fruit of itself, except it abide in the vine; no more can ye, except ye abide in Me."

Now, whatever we find to be the true idea of the union between the vine and the branches, that will be at least one fact in the union between the believer and Christ. It will illustrate at one point what is meant by being "in Christ."

Studying then the vine and branches, first of all we see that the branches *live in the vine*. They derive all their life from it. Taking then the believer as a branch, we must find his life in Christ. Now this certainly does not mean his natural life, though it is perfectly true that this is from Christ, but he has another life. He is a new creature. He has what is peculiarly a believer's life—the life which makes him a Christian. It is a life which makes him a new creature, if he ever lived in worldliness and sin; and if not, it makes him a new creature in contrast with the men of the world all about him. Now this new life is the life which he derives from Christ.

At this point two ideas at once arise : (I.) The origin of this life; and (II.) The sustenance of it, as both are from Christ.

(I.) Now, as to the first there are two ways in which this new life may originate, and the figure of the vine and branches is a correct symbol, whether we refer to the one origin or the other.

1. First, then, this new life may begin with a person's natural life. Born in sin indeed, every one is met at the gates of life by the benefit of the work of Christ—a free gift—putting him right with God, and enabling him to begin to live with all the Holy Spirit's power anointing him for the new life. This is all suggested indeed by the branches and the vine. The branches generally have never existed but in the vine. They had their natural origin in it, and have grown with it steadily in the progress of its growth. Now, here we have a suggestion concerning Christian children. May they be in Christ from their earliest years just as the branches are in the vine? Assuredly. This is God's idea of Christian nurture. What we call conversion is simply the beginning of a Christian course in life, but if one could be in this course from his earliest years, why need he know anything about this beginning? He would have begun to live in this way before he knew that there was any other way. There are many such persons. It was a revelation to them when at five or six or ten years of age they discovered that any one lived without prayer, or that any one hated God instead of loving Him.

We are diffident about accepting this as possible because we feel very modest about our success with our own children. But we may undervalue the good our effort has been to our children. Let us see what Christian nurture has done for the average child of our homes and our Sunday Schools. They have as a result of it :

(1) A good general knowledge of the scriptural truth involved in a Christian profession, and also of the duties required in it.

(2) They have at heart all the rudimentary principles of Christian morality, and they preserve at least a good outline of it in practice.

(3) Their prejudices are so instructed that they all favor true religion. Its battle is their battle.

(4) They retain the habit of prayer and feelings of reverence. Again and again I have gone through large Sabbath School classes with the question, " Do you pray ?" and in ninety-nine cases out of a hundred the answer is " Yes."

(5) Then they have as much faith in Jesus as the converts on the day of Pentecost had.

Now the nurture which has produced these results has not been a failure by any means. The objects of it still lack, in that—

(1) Their application of Christ to their own lives is not perfect.

(2) They do not make any open profession of Him as their own Saviour and leader.

But what they have goes incalculably farther than what they lack. More wisdom in teaching, and less bondage to the idea of a sort of mechanical conversion, from which they gather that they may not be Christians until they have experi-

enced a great physical excitement corresponding
to some other person's conversion, would bring
these children happily under the bond of a personal profession of Christ. Then they would feel
that they are Christians because Christ lets them
be, and their new life would date its origin correctly with the origin of the natural life.

2. But this new life may originate in another
way, and that is by grafting. Many branches in
a vine may have been engrafted upon it. There
are several processes, as budding, etc., but I will
only refer to the more common method of grafting.
In this —

(1) First the old branch is cut completely off. It
must not be left attached by any portion of the
wood and bark. This illustrates the last clause of
the text, " Old things are passed away." This was
true in the case of every convert when Paul wrote.
Jewish law or pagan ceremonies and superstitions
all disappeared from the convert's faith and practice. It was a thorough emptying out. Now, it is
not true of many Christian children. It would be
found true somewhere in their family history if
you went back far enough, but it is not true in
their personal history. Then there is

(2) The insertion of this new scion, or the life
that is to control the fruit which is to be borne.

Now the new life originates by this engrafting
process in all cases where there is a marked conversion from sin to holiness. In all great revivals the

multitudes brought to the Saviour are branches engrafted into the vine.

There is a tendency to envy this type of conversion. This is an error. The gardener gives much attention to the grafting process. For a time his labor is expended more upon these new scions than upon the branches which are bearing good fruit. So we desire revivals. It is always the old story over again of the prodigal son and his elder brother. Note then—

(1) The weakness of the new scion ; and

(2) The importance of its subsequent growth and development ; and also

(3) That the branches which did not need to be replaced by engrafting are really the most valuable to the gardener. He loses not the product of their fruit for several years while the new scion is growing large enough to bear.

(II.) We come now to the second of the ideas suggested by the derivation of life from Christ by the believer, as the branch deriving its life from the vine, that is, the sustenance of this new life.

Now this is equally from Christ as the origin of it was. The branch depends upon the vine every moment. There is a circulation of the sap from the remotest root fibre up to the smallest twig, and through every trembling leaf. This circulation constantly feeds the life in every part and causes growth. Pluck away a leaf, cut down a branch, and in a little time it is withered, dry, and dead. It cannot live if cut off from its support in the vine.

No more can the Christian if cut off from Christ. His new life is hidden with Christ. It feeds upon Him. It is not of the world. It cannot run with it. It must be separate. Sometimes streams in which the water of one is darker than that in the other flow together in the same channel. The dividing line can be traced for a long distance down after they join. A noticeable case of this kind is that of the two rivers in Switzerland, the Rhone and the Aarve. The waters of Lake Leman are of a beautiful, transparent, deep blue color. Their outlet is the Rhone river, into whose channel they rush like a torrent. The Aarve is fed by melting glaciers, which grind along the rocks in the mountain side, breaking and crushing them, and the sediment mingles with the water until it seems like liquid mortar rushing through its narrow channel. When they meet, the waters will not mingle. The pure, virgin waters of the Rhone refuse to be contaminated by the touch of so vile a consort. And so, as far as the eye can see, they flow on side by side without mingling, and tourists go out to look at the remarkable spectacle. Those waters represent the life of the Christian and the life of the world flowing on side by side. They must touch each other as long as human life beats the earth in its onward march, but they cannot intermingle. They can never be one, because they flow from different sources. Refine the world and sin as you will, you cannot make of them piety toward God. Refined worldli-

ness is not religion. If any one tries to blend
these two he goes himself over into the stream of
worldliness.

Stand again beside the channel into which those
two Swiss rivers have flown. If a ton or more
of the blue water goes over into the grey, muddy
water, it is at once absorbed and lost without
making any impression. The grey water is no more
pure because of it. But if a ton of the foul water
should go over into the blue, it could be clearly
traced there. It would not be absorbed and lost as
in the former case. So true religion loses itself
when it mixes with worldliness. All idea of eleva-
ting the world to religion by going into its ways is
a delusion. The Christian will be dragged down
and lost, but the world will not be drawn up to
prayer and duty and self-sacrifice. And when, on
the other hand, worldliness runs over into the
Church, it shows itself there. It is not absorbed
and lost. It does not become good by association.
A worldly Church is easily known.

Let, then, the world go its way. It is not Christ;
it is not of Him. But the Christian has a peculiar
life, the support of which is his constant communion with Christ. The leaf cut off from the tree
dies. So the Christian cut off from Christ ceases to
live the peculiar life of a Christian. Let him lose
the all-pervading persuasion of Christ's great love;
let him forget the sacrifice by which he was redeemed; let him cease to dwell upon Christ as an

ever present, loving, helping friend; let him no
longer pray unto Christ, and so touch Him with his
own throbbing heart—his spiritual life is gone. He
is no longer in the true sense a Christian. He
may retain the outward forms of religion and the
services of morality, but he is a dead leaf, cut off
from the vine and lying upon the ground.

What then is the source and origin of our religion? Is it a union with Christ? Are we in
Him in the sense of having a life derived at first
from Him, and still constantly sustained by Him?
Or have we a religion because it is fashionable?
because we desire greater influence than we could
have without it? or because by it we gain admission into better society? Oh, let us be sure about
this. Let us have a religion which is, indeed, life
in Christ. A religion of refined, exquisite worldliness will never tide us over great swelling waves
of sorrow, nor bear us up in death's dark hour.

II. I mention, second, that to be in Christ is to be
united to Him for perfect service, by our undivided
faculties and energies.

This truth is set forth in the figure which represents Christ as a human body, and the Christian
people as the members of which this body is composed. (See 1 Cor. xii. from 20th verse to end.)

Now, here are three ideas:

1. Each member is in the body, no matter how
humble. Every true member of the Church may
say, "For me to live is Christ," no matter how

humble he is. There is a difference, certainly, in the dignity of the different members of the body. Yet every one can claim identity with the man. Take the most honored man on earth. Take his least toe—that is so little honored that you at first think it is a little vulgar even to mention it here— yet it can lift itself up and say, "I am the King or President." The finger-nail even may say the same. So may any hair which the next minute will be caught in the wind and carried away. Let us remember this. No matter where in the Church we serve, we are still of the body, and may say, "For me to live is Christ."

Some members are very useful. Dr. North's man, "Terry," at Clifton Springs Sanitarium, attending men in bathing, remarked about the human hand as made different from the termination of the forearm in any other animal. "Made to assist," he said. He had for years done nothing but help men in the various baths, but this observation had taught him that much Christianity. As by an object lesson he had learned that men are made to serve.

The blind preacher, Milburn, told Dr. Nelles that he would rather be blind than deaf. The ear opened the soul to the highest harmonies, the music of the human voice, the words of friendship and love, the currents of active thought and intelligence. He would rather be left in darkness to imagine the beauties of the inanimate world than to have his soul closed up against the currents of living thought.

But after all, the eye is a most honored member. It is the anointed teacher of the man. It is his heaven-lighted sun ; his lamp to guide.

It is certainly grand to be an eye or ear in the Church. The eye receives revelations for the whole man. To stand like Moses and Elijah on awful Horeb's top, and receive the unfolding revelations, whether on tables of stone graven by the finger of God, or in the voices of the unimaginable thunder robed in wide, expanding sheets of flame, while the furious night strides across trembling heights? Oh ! it is glorious thus, as an eye, to receive revelations from God ; and it is no less glorious to be an apostolic hand, shaking the bars of prisons while jailors sleep, and in one's own blood to lay the foundations of new systems that shall lead the civilization of coming ages. But what if we may not rise to such distinguished service ? Life is short, and the best and highest that any man can gain or reach, either in the Church or the world, is neither great nor very eminent. But if Christ will take the cup of cold water given in love to a fainting fellow-man as given to Him ; if He will esteem the cool hand laid upon the fevered brow of a sick child, as laid upon His pierced and bleeding brow, aching and throbbing in an agony of pain ; if the melting compassion that hands bread to the hungry feeds His famished body fainting and falling upon the mountain path ; if the stooping tenderness that weeps in a prison cell with the condemned criminal over his bitterly lamented crime is poured into His heart, breaking under the burden of the whole world's sorrow; oh, then, the grandest eminence I can reach is to give up my feet to run on errands of mercy for Him; my hands to lift the burdens from His pierced and bleeding hands; my tongue to speak words of sympathy to Him to whom none spoke words of sympathy in His hours of deepest darkness.

2. Another comforting idea is that all these members serve equally. In verses 28 and 29, there is a distribution of various offices. What we are to notice is that those offices only mean different kinds of service, to which different characters were adapted by nature. They were not dignities. The most perfect equality prevailed among the members of the early Church. They were all of the priesthood. The Jewish idea of a wide division between the priests and the people had been succeeded by a Church in which every member was a priest consecrated to God. Anyone might equally with another take the lead in the sacrament.

If then we are in Christ, we shall equally serve in Japan or among the Indians, or as the teacher of the humblest class, or by the bed of the sick, or nursing a child, or scouring in the kitchen. This we claim if holiness is to be written upon the pots. (Zechariah xiv. 20, 21.)

3. The third idea is that service does appropriately represent the union between Christ and the Chris-

tian. Service is the true idea of sanctification. Entire service is entire sanctification. (Romans xii. 1,
2.) The body is perfectly sanctified by being perfectly given up to God. It is not changed by
the Holy Spirit. The first verse represents the
sanctification of the body, and the second that of
the mind.

There are several planes of experience. One is
that of "I'm saved." Many in religious meetings
never speak of anything else.

Well, why not say that over and over? At that
stage there is nothing else or better to say. Some
ridicule the hymn, "I love Jesus, I love Jesus."
But what else is there to say if not to say this over
and over again?

A higher stage. Go to one of our charitable
homes, and you will not find it saying, "I feel," but it
will show a world of experience. Is the tear which
falls because the Home for Incurables is not large
enough to receive all applicants, or because some
ragged boy, an orphan, cannot gain admittance to
the Boys' Home, not as much an evidence of sanctification as the ability to talk of being made very
happy?

I have no fear of losing heaven if I can have the
sanctification which is proven by perfect service.
I do not any more think about my getting into
heaven at all. I do think about making my life so
pure and good that it will be helpful and will appear
religious also. The getting me into heaven is God's

business, not mine. Indeed, if I do my utmost I do not even know if I care whether He takes me to heaven or not. I know what Wesley says about "servant" and "son." I despise a religion, call it holiness, or sanctification, or what you will, which does not make a man's life full of fruitfulness, so that poverty because of him is less bitter, and sickness is less painful, and death less dark and lonely.

III. The believer is in Christ as the different stones are in a building. In illustration of this, see Eph. ii. 19-22; 1 Peter ii. 5; 1 Cor. iii. 16.

Here is a double metaphor. Christians are a household—the household of Christ. But the household must inhabit a house. Therefore Christians are a house. But if we take it as a simple metaphor, we get at strictly correct ideas of truth.

This figure sets forth several thoughts.

1. Each believer is one stone in a great building.

Then the Christian in this world is simply a stonedresser in a vast stoneyard, where many are laboring, each upon his own piece. When the Windsor Hotel was building, great blocks were imported, from twelve to sixteen feet long, and were dressed into fluted, round and square columns. Men stood around them and admired; but the workman was engaged upon his own piece and thought little of the plan of the whole great building.

So the Christian's interest lies in the working out of his own character.

7

Now in this stoneyard of the world there are at least three kinds of workmen. I go where they are building the great Parliament Buildings in the park, and talk with the men dressing the blocks of stone to be built into the walls. I ask this man, " What are you doing ? " He says, " I am working for $1.50 a day, sir." Now that man represents those whose idea of life is simply to get as much money as they can. " What are you doing ? " " Oh, I made $10,000, $20,000, or $100,000 last year." That is what they are doing.

Take the next man. " What are you doing ? " " I am dressing this block of granite, sir. It is to go into the Parliament Buildings. I don't know where, but I am dressing it according to the pattern drawn out on this piece of paper." Now he represents a Christian whose life is not filled with the money he makes. His thought takes a higher range. He lives for what he can make of himself. What is he doing ? He is trying to keep the image of God in his own soul, to lift his character up by the imitation of all that is grand and noble ; but he is not the highest type of a Christian.

I pass on to the third workman and I ask, " What are you doing ? " Note, these three are working upon blocks just alike in size and pattern. This third man replies, " I am helping to make the great Parliament Buildings." Now, there is a Christian, but he is one whose views have a higher range than even the former. His thoughts are not confined to the single piece of work he has in hand at present. They range over the whole vast and grand structure of which he is shaping only an humble part. He has seen not only the plan of his own character, but God's great plan for the world.

A few can thus enter into God's great plans. It makes life certainly more easy, and doubtless more noble.

But the Christian who cannot work thus is still able to work upon his own piece. He can keep himself. He doubtless will talk chiefly about his conversion, his sanctification, his temptations and trials and hopes. All this is individual. It is only stone dressing, but it is necessary. As you can have no grand buildings without stone dressing, so you can have no grand structure of society without the dressing of individual character.

Some people look so much at the plan that they do not dress their own stone. So are those who talk about the progress of civilization, and the onward movement of the race; and they themselves have neither faith nor love. My father told me to hold the light so that I could see what he was doing. I couldn't understand what he did, especially in making the many slats for the shutters of our new house, I never having seen a slatted shutter. His words come to me now. Christianity says, "See what I am doing." I look, and lo, pagan nations are rising into the light of the gospel. I look again, and lo, poverty is fed, orphanage no longer weeps, sorrow's tears are dried.

2. A second thought is that the architect places each of these stones in its place. No stone knows where it is to go, until by the plan the builder begins to place them together. " To whom coming." " In whom ye are also builded together." My character concerns myself; my place in relation to the whole, concerns the architect. I am not to think much about what the great building will be, but I should think constantly about what I myself shall be in character. My duty is to bring out the utmost in beauty and worth in myself. He will give to each his place in the temple here and hereafter according as it pleases Him. The true stone thinks not whether he shall be a highly figured stone to adorn the cornice toward which all eyes shall turn in admiration, or shall be a huge block made to endure for ages lying away down in the foundations, out of sight, but supporting the whole; whether a turned and fluted column he shall stand boldly out in the portico, or with rough jagged edges, buried up within the walls, he shall give strength and body to the whole side of the building. If he can be sure that he is where the architect wills, it is of little consequence to him where or how the years of his life be spent. In our great Parliament Buildings, at Ottawa, the stone which reflects more glory upon the great pile than any other is the foundation stone laid by the Prince of Wales when passing through the country in 1860. It bears an inscription commemorating the event. But the

average visitor never sees that stone. It is away
down in the basement, and is reached through long
and dark passages wholly uninteresting, and no
one would ever think of going there unless guided
by some one familiar with the place. So it is in
Christ's great building. Often some obscure stone,
spending its life down in some dark passage, is most
precious to Christ.

But some one must be first. Even in the Church
some stone must rest on the giddy and dangerous
summit, and it may be, as indeed it ought to be,
more gracious than the most obscure; only we
will make sure that if we are in Christ, our only
thought is for the glory of His whole body, not the
fame of ourselves; the splendor of the whole house,
not the attention paid to us as a particular stone in
it; and if we can be sure that this is our spirit, then
we will have proof that we are in Christ no matter
how high up we may climb.

We must remember that we cannot always, or
even often, understand the greatness of God's designs.
The universe of life is worth more to God than any
individual in the world. True, the hairs of your
head are all numbered; but God is great enough to
work on grander plans than those contained in any
human life. He moves toward a redeemed race.
The idols shall be all broken down. Wrong and
fraud shall come to an end. Truth and righteousness shall be stamped upon every brow. All tears
shall be wiped from all faces. The earth shall

keep jubilee together.   Universal rest and peace shall reign.

3. A third thought is that this house so built is a temple. " Unto an holy temple in the Lord." " Ye are the temple of the Lord." " Ye also as lively stones are built up a spiritual house." That is, if the whole building is consecrated, then every stone in it is consecrated, and every part of the life of every stone.   All of every saint's life is to be service and praise,—the office, the parlor, the ship.   Do nothing if not sure that it is acceptable to God.   All must be as fit for temple service as song, and prayer, and sacrament.

It will follow, that to be in Christ is,

1. To be personally holy. " Holiness becometh thine house, O Lord."

2. To be surrendered wholly to His glory.   After all the beautifully-dressed pieces in the Parliament Buildings were put in their appropriate places, I do not suppose that since the splendid front was completed, any one has ever in passing along, given himself up completely to the contemplation of any particular stone ; but again and again men have said, " What a splendid building !"   They have admired the structure as a whole.   Each stone actually surrendered its beauty, and lost its individuality in contributing to the beauty of the whole.

3. He is safe in Christ.

A MAN IS MADE BY WHAT HE THINKS ABOUT.

"Think on these things."—PHIL. iv. 8.

L ET us first of all recognize the fact that one must think about something. A stream flows without either knowing it or intending it. The wind blows without any purpose or plan, and so a man's thoughts rush on, leaping from one thing to another, whether he will or no. It is the result of both nature and habit that the human mind shall constantly have some manner of thoughts passing through it. When it is not under any control it just drifts along like a stick in a stream, striking upon whatever happens to be in the way. If you could gather together every image that passes over the mind in an hour, what a motley assemblage there would be! And how many that no one would willingly own as the children of his will! No one would say concerning them, "I intended to think that." But they exist, because if the mind be not of a set purpose, filled with good thoughts, it will of itself catch upon something that is passing, and it may be rude or grotesque, or even vile. And it is because

it is much easier to allow the mind to drift in its
own way than to direct it that we find it difficult to
read a book and keep ourselves intent upon what
it contains, or to listen to a sermon without distrac-
tion. Take the hour spent in this service. How
hard to keep everything out of our minds but hymn
and prayer and lesson and sermon! How often we
sit the hour through without getting one distinct
impression from the service! It is because our
minds will constantly have some thoughts, and it
is easier to allow them to catch up whatever comes
than to confine them to what is properly brought
before them.

II. Let us pass on to consider that a person has
it in his power to determine what he will think
about. Certainly the Bible teaches that men have
this power. The text plainly implies that a man
can think upon certain things if he chooses to do so.
Then there is the exhortation, "Keep thy heart
with all diligence." This means that a man can
control his thoughts. It certainly means more than
that; but this it does mean, that though difficult,
yet it is possible for anyone to decide of what manner his thoughts shall be. The same is implied in
that discourse of our Lord (Matt. xv.) which teaches
that it is not what enters into the mouth but what
comes out of the heart that defiles a man, for out of
the heart proceed evil thoughts.

We also find in experience that men do determine
their own habitual thoughts. Take five sons of the

same parents. They are brought up and educated in as nearly the same manner as children in one family can be. One of these sons goes into mercantile life. In a short time his habitual thoughts are of the various goods and articles used in daily life by the masses of men. He thinks about markets, scales of profit, the laws of trade, competition, and such like things. Another becomes a manufacturer, and his thoughts run wholly upon wants and their supply, upon the creation of new wants and machinery, upon importations of materials, and exportation of implements. Another enters politics, and he soon thinks of nothing but parties and places and elections, and the management of rivals and of the masses of the people. One becomes a minister and is full of theology and the exposition of Scripture, and of the moral and spiritual life of men. The fifth is a sailor, and thinks of cargoes and storms, and ports and distant lands, and latitudes and longitudes. Now, did each of these men come involuntarily upon his current of habitual thought, in each so different from that in every other, or was it the result of his own choice? Most assuredly he determined for himself upon what thoughts his mind should be most engaged during his life.

But that is on a large scale. By choosing a certain pursuit, without any thought about the habits it will necessarily form, he determines in one act the habitual thoughts of a lifetime. That is true enough. But what is true on a large scale is also

true on a small one. Either of these men might
have chosen some other profession. And so on any
day or hour he may turn out one thought and take
up another by an act of his will. We are doing this
all the time. You see your boy leave the music, or
the attractive games and conversation in the parlor,
and go away to his own quiet room alone. He says,
" I have my to-morrow's lessons to get up." A man
rises from the comfortable surroundings of his draw-
ing-room, and the attractive company of his wife
and children, and goes away saying, " I have an
engagement on business." What is the fact in either
of these cases but that the individual determines
to put some thoughts out of his mind, and to put
others in ? Every person who has tried to live a
pure and spotless life knows that again and again he
does force some thoughts out of his mind and bring
others in. In fact we are doing it all the time. It
is only when we are disposed to soothe our conscience, and yet indulge ourselves in idle dreaming,
or worse still, in covetous, or even foul and lustful
imaginings, that we say we cannot determine what
thoughts we will have. A man will perhaps indulge
himself in lewd thoughts, and say he cannot help it ;
but if his clerk or errand boy spends the time
dreaming when he ought to be applying himself,
that same man will treat him as though he had perfect power to think of what he will and of what he
ought. We feel and acknowledge this power with
regard to each other, but only doubt it in relation

to God. This much only may be said. We cannot keep any thought from obtruding into our minds, but we can prevent its remaining there. A burglar may enter our house unknown to us; but we have power to arise and drive him out. So it is with our thoughts.

III. Notice now that what a person thinks about will determine what his character and acts will be. The habitual thoughts give their color and impress to a man's whole character. They make him like themselves, and determine the value of everything he does in life. Homer sang his "Iliad." It was adapted to the civilization of the time, a story of battles and heroes; a picture of passion, and plunder and blood. Alexander, afterwards called the Great, read it, and the images of that poem lived in his mind and became the subject of his habitual thoughts, intensified by the example of his great and warlike father. The result was that Alexander conceived and carried out the grandest schemes of war, bloodshed and conquest that the world has ever yet seen. Then in turn, his great career wrought upon the mind of the Roman, Julius Cæsar, who brooded over that picture of martial pomp, and victory and glory, until he rushed into the same bloody stream, and thinking of victories on the field and triumphs at Rome, devoted himself to a life of slaughter and oppression. And Charles XII. of Sweden, from the same source derived a similar inspiration, and in acts of a like nature

wrought out the problem of his earthly existence.
This law holds good everywhere.   Two boys
receive the same education.   They enter upon the
same calling in life—say, that of an engineer.   One
thinks only of profit, the money that repays his skill
and toil.   The other is constantly thinking of a more
perfect application of mechanical laws, how he may
raise great weights with the least tax upon human
strength, how he may most easily remove vast
masses of matter.   It requires no deep wisdom to
discern how widely the character of the two will
differ in ten years' time, and upon what widely
differing works their skill will be employed.

Some think that the surroundings and not the
thoughts determine character.   John Ruskin tells of
a man, a great philosopher indeed, who travelled all
day upon the lake of Geneva.   His mind was
absorbed upon some favorite subject and he saw
nothing.   At night he asked where Lake Leman
(Geneva) was.   Certainly surroundings did not make
his character.   In what does the man Cetewayo,
the Zulu King, differ from an English statesman ?
Why only in his thoughts.   The English people
expected to see in him a naked savage.   But before
he entered the kingdom they dressed him in the
uniform of an English soldier.   He received that
change into his thoughts, and by so much he became
an Englishman.   Now suppose he had stayed in
England long enough for all his thoughts to have
become the same as an Englishman's thoughts, he
would no longer have been a mere savage.

If a person does not subject his thoughts to any control, but allows them to drift at random, his character will be weak, his acts will have little force, or energy, or inspiration in them, his life will be made up of words and acts of the lowest form, chiefly of a routine character, his hands doing and his tongue saying just what they have learned to do and say as a habit. But where great and noble thoughts throb in the mind, they are sure to burn their way out, and blaze forth in grand and thrilling words, and throw upon the surface of life far reaching acts charged with the destiny of men and of nations—such as live in men's memories forever! A man's thoughts always make him what he is.

IV. Let us now see what thoughts make the truest and best character. "Think on these things." The things mentioned are such as are honest, true, just, pure, lovely, of good report, virtue, praise. These are the leading Christian virtues— the sum of all true morality and purity.

1. Let a person think much of the intrinsic excellence of these things. Gold is the most costly of metals. But in a land where there is no commerce, and therefore no need of a medium of exchange, gold would have very little value. Or even in a land where it is so abundant as to be picked up everywhere, it would have no value. But iron has an intrinsic value. However abundant, there are many things for which it is absolutely necessary. Men could hardly get along

without it. So it is of "these things." They are
of value in themselves. Take the morality you
cultivate because it is necessary to get you into
good society, take the honesty you cherish, because
honesty is the best policy, the truth you speak,
because falsehood is sure to get entangled in its
own ropes.

Myself and a friend were conversing about
modesty, and noting how well some men pushed
themselves forward by pure force of impudence.
"But" said he, "a man must keep his modesty for
his own sake. A time will come when each person
will be a complete man on the plan he has chosen,
and no one at that time can afford to be without
any good thing in his character."

2. Think much of the effect of these things on
one's self.

3. Think much of their effect upon society. A
man is on a low plane indeed who makes himself
only the burden of his thoughts, even though the
chief thought be the salvation of his own soul.
Everyone is bound to think somewhat of the good
he may do to others, and the influence he may leave
behind him. But truth, honesty, justice and purity
are the chief pillars on which society depends.
Without them, love, the great bond of union among
men, cannot exist. Take them out and let men
feel that there is no honesty or truth in voluntary
transactions, and no justice in public affairs, and
no purity in the social intercourse of life, what

have you left ? *Savagery.* The civilized man has given up the thoughts of civilization and Christianity, and has taken up the thoughts of the savage. The name of the enlightened state may remain, but the plunder and lust, and fraud and wrong of the savage condition wholly prevail. History tells of the Northern barbarians having overrun the Empire of Rome, and brought the world back to the savage state. Why, the fact is that Rome under the Empire had retrograded from its former civilization and had become barbarian. Goth and Vandal, in the days of the overthrow of the Empire, were as civilized as the Roman himself. Rome had ceased to have the thoughts of honesty, truth and justice and purity which make up a civilized state, and had all the thoughts of plunder and fraud and lust of falsehood that belong to the savage.

4. Again think of the obligation to God to cultivate these virtues. They are of God. They are God-like. As we cultivate them we become like Him.

V. These are the thoughts which the religion of Christ puts into a man's mind. No one can feel that strongest of controlling influences, the love of Christ, without finding that the thought of these things fills him. Religion is the only thing that can keep possession of a man's thoughts all the time. But how about the duties of life, business, society ? This is explained in two ways.

1. These thoughts are just the thoughts that belong to business and society.

2. When a man turns from business his danger begins. If he can keep truth and honesty while at work, he still has the care of things pure, lovely, of good report, afterwards. Two men are engaged upon their book accounts, straightening and balancing their affairs. One is an infidel and blasphemer, guilty of transgressing every law of the decalogue, the other a pure-minded, honest, true, earnest Christian. But in that work, for the time being, one is as good as the other. But they cease, for rest, for a night, for a holiday. Now the difference between them appears in what they do in that interval or break in regular duty. Settlers fill up a township or county. They build their houses upon elevated places, and cultivate the dry lands. These give them no trouble. But a marsh lies along the whole side of the county. Everyone thinks about the drainage and redemption of that waste, for all know that it will breed fevers. All are concerned to save themselves from the waste. So in life.

THE SINGLE EYE, THE SIMPLE INTENTION.

"The light of the body is the eye ; if therefore thine eye be single, thy whole body shall be full of light. But if thine eye be evil, thy whole body shall be full of darkness."—MATT. vi. 22, 23.

THIS is a strong metaphor, "If thine eye be single," that is, if it be whole, or well, or in perfect health. In that case it will see objects naturally and as they are. Or it may also be taken to mean if the eye be fixed steadily upon one definite point, there will be no confusion in the impression received. The object will be distinctly discerned. When in either of these senses the eye is single, the "whole body is full of light." That means that each portion of the body acts and performs its part as well as if it were itself an eye. The traveller looks along the path in which he desires to go, and his feet walk straight on in that path. They keep to it as well as if they saw it for themselves. The builder sees the nail he would hit, and the hand brings the blow down upon it with as much precision as if the hand itself saw the nail. The eye takes in the true condition of things, and the tongue speaks words appropriate to that condition. It is the

S

student who finds his library all in confusion, and his tongue directs that order be restored. It is a lady who meets one child crying in the street, and speaks words of comfort and encouragement to him; but seeing another breaking a window, she warns him that he will be punished for his trespass. Truly when the eye sees correctly, every part of the body does its special work as well as if each organ saw for itself. "The whole body is full of light." This is something which we are proving in the experience of every day. It is so common that we have to stop and think before we can realize the fact.

But now, what if the eye be evil? This means diseased. In some affections of the eye it sees things double. Sometimes it cannot fix correctly the distance of an object from the observer, or, perhaps, it is impossible to keep it bent steadily upon any one thing. It is all the time roving from one thing to another. Under these circumstances the whole body is full of darkness. Its movements will be unsteady, or they will not be directed as though the person understood the real condition of things. The hand will move as if it does not know what it wants to touch, or it will strike at a man who is perfectly innocent, mistaking him for another near by who is guilty of some offence. The tongue will begin a sentence in one vein and end it in another, or it will upbraid a sick man for not being at work. It will accuse a man of drunkenness when he is perfectly sober. Certainly such words appear as if the tongue

could not see. It is in total darkness when it speaks
so far aside from what the circumstances justify.
And so in equal darkness the foot will begin to walk
towards one object, and will bring up at another.
When the eye is thus out of health, there is no even-
ness in any movements of the body. The person
seems like one who does not know what he wants to
do, or who does not know his own mind. All the
way through, the body is like one who has no guiding light. The whole body is full of darkness, because the eye is not right.

Now, this is the physical side of this metaphor.
But it has a spiritual side. What is there in our
moral or spiritual life that may be taken as the ana-
logue to the facts just described ? It is plain that
the eye stands for the intentions of the heart. A
man's intentions are to his soul what the eye is to
the body. This statement has very strong support.
In one sermon Mr. Wesley says, " The eye is the intention ; what the eye is to the body, the intention
is to the soul." (Sermons, Vol. I., 256 p.) He must
have said this upon thorough conviction, and as a
settled truth with him, for in another sermon he
says, "What the eye is to the body, that the intention is to all the words and actions." (Sermons, Vol.
I., 104 p.) Dr. Adam Clark gives us the same idea.
He says : " Our blessed Lord uses the sound eye as
a metaphor to point out simplicity of intention."

If then we are to carry out in the spiritual life
the figure of the eye used in this text, we must

begin with a single intention. The meaning of the passage is better expressed by the word simple. It is the same idea conveyed by the Latin *simplex*, that is, unmixed, uncompounded, simple, as when a chemist speaks of a simple substance, or a musician of a simple sound.

This intention must be directed wholly towards God. It is an eye that looks only toward heaven, and wishes only to gain it. Now, such an intention must be wholly good. There can be no admixture of evil in it. It needs no apology. It is insulted and wronged by any defence.

It is quite unnecessary to start any question as to such an intention being followed by appropriate conduct. It is impossible that it be otherwise. It must be followed by appropriate conduct. Talk about the contrary! As well talk about a fountain not being followed by any stream, or a railroad terminus not having any railroad, or a mother's love not followed by any gifts to her child. There would never be an act in the world if it were not for an intention preceding it. The intention creates the act. The intention is the end for which the act exists, as the terminus is the end of a railroad, or good gifts are the fruit of affection. So this simple intention will, without fail, throw up out of itself acts of its own nature. It will lead the whole life in obedience to itself. A rope-walker fixes his eye upon some point before him, and the eye controls his step, and keeps him steady. Some can never walk over a stream, or upon a high wall. Others can walk as well in such a place as over the face of a broad prairie. The secret is wholly in what they look at. No person could walk in these places if he looked down, or around him ; he must fix his attention upon one point, and his whole movement will tend toward that spot.

So let a Christian have a simple intention. Let it keep his thought turned toward God and heaven, and he will be, with regard to such works as lie in the road to heaven, or which a man going to heaven ought to perform, like one whose eye is sound, and whose whole body is full of light. His conduct will all be like that of a man who is more intent upon gaining heaven than upon realizing anything that this world can give. Each separate act will seem to be done with the aim and intention of getting to heaven. There is a separate intention for each individual act, but these intentions take their character from the one ruling intention of the man's life.

> " All motives bowing to one leadership,
> And aiding its emprise, are one with it—
> The same in trend, the same in terminus.
> All the low motives that obey the law,
> And aid the work of one above them all,
> Do holy service, and fulfil the end
> For which they were designed."

Now, this is just the case with an earnest Christian man. The one strong, simple aim or intention of his life exercises a controlling influence, and the distinct intention out of which each separate act springs into being has its character from that original ruling intention. As in a general way he intends to live for God, so in each act he intends to live for God.

The consequence of this is that he is like one whose body is full of light. All his acts are as if in beginning each one of them, he had suddenly and just then conceived the idea of pleasing God.

The result is that in God's sight they are perfect. To Him they are as if perfectly done. Defects of body and mind may cause many things which he does to appear far from what they ought to be, but in the judgment of heaven they are just what they were intended to be, and that is perfect. Is not this true ? Was not Abraham esteemed by God as if he had actually offered up Isaac ? Did not David receive commendation the same as if he had built the temple ? How about the widow who could give only two mites? And Mary who only poured a box of precious ointment upon her Lord's head ? Did not God hold each of these as worthy as if they had actually accomplished all that their love prompted them to do ? Assuredly He did.

And men in their best moments also give a man credit for all the good he intended to do. A poor farmer gave a dish of cold water to Artaxerxes, the Persian king. Now, that was not much to do, but the king saw in the act a love that would be willing

to do much greater things, and he rewarded the poor
man with the gift of a golden goblet. You remember that more than five hundred years ago the English king took Calais, after a siege of a year. He
offered to spare the lives of the citizens if six of
their chief men would come out to the city's gate,
with a halter upon each neck, and surrender to him,
to be immediately executed. Six of the first citizens so came out to him, and but for the kind inter-
cession of a queen, less barbarous than her husband,
this monstrous sentence would have been inflicted.
They were ordered to death, but the queen came on
just in time to save them. The men did not die, but
has not history honored them as if they had actually
died ? Have not children wept over them with the
same sympathy as if they had been cruelly put to
death, as they expected to be when they went out
to the city's gate ? And so all the time we are giving our children and our friends full credit for what
they intend to do. And this is what God does when
our intention is simple.

II. But we advance now to find the spiritual
meaning of the other side of this metaphor. "If
thine eye be evil thy whole body is full of darkness." It is reasonable to take this as meaning just
the opposite of the previous clause, with which we
have been dealing. A diseased eye seeing double,
or in some other way deranged, is to the body what
conflicting intentions are to the soul. As the single
eye means a simple intention or an unmixed aim, so
the evil eye means a mixture of intentions.

A number of times when standing in this place, I have said that the intention which gives birth to an act is either all good, or else wholly bad. The same act cannot have a parentage partly good, and partly evil. You will notice that this text supports my statement. If an intention is unmixed, and is fully fixed upon God, then it is wholly good, and it makes the act that springs from it good also. But if the intention be mixed, - that is, the meaning for that is directly opposite to simple,—then it is evil. A mixture of intentions is evil, and that is all there is about it. The word here calls it evil without any manner of qualification. This must end the case.

Now, a little thought upon this matter will show that it is perfectly reasonable that mixed intentions should be counted as evil. Take this simple illustration of the case. Ask your boy, who is just beginning to study geometry, to try if he can draw two distinct straight lines between any two given points. At first thought he will say, "Yes, I can; of course I can." Very likely you would say the same thing, if you had not thought upon it. Well, let the boy get about the work. Study the results. He may make two lines between any two points easily enough, but one will be straight, and the other curved, or both will be curved. There cannot possibly be more than one right line between two given points. Well now, mixed intentions are like two straight lines trying to lie between the same two points. Exam-

ine these mixed intentions, as we call them.   A man
has a general intention to live for God, and to be an
acceptable Christian.   Now that is all right.   That
can be only good.   But he gets into some speculation.   He holds the big end of the stick in his own
hand.   He has a splendid chance, such a one as will
probably never come to him again.   He thinks that
it would be too bad not to make a big haul, especially as it is his only opportunity.   True, it will not
be strictly honest, but the fact is when once he gets
the money into his hands he will give very largely of
it to support his church.   Now, this is a very fair
specimen of a mixed intention.   Take another case.
There is as before, the general purpose to live as a
Christian, and to please God.   But some fascinating
pleasure has cast its thrall over the man.   It will
not be long; it will be only once.   Of course the
pleasure is forbidden by the Bible, and by all that is
best in our natures.   But then one would like to
know just what it is for only once, and so he yields,
and wilfully does what he knows God forbids.   Now
this is another example, and a very common one, of
a mixed intention.   Some speak of these, and other
similar examples, as being cases of mixed intention,
where what one intends to do is partly good and
partly evil.   I do not think that this is correct.
There are two ways of describing the entanglement,
without calling it a mixed intention, partly good,
and partly bad.   The way which puts it in the best
light, is to allow that in these cases there are two

intentions lying across each other.   There is a general intention to be a Christian, always good.   Then
just at the time of action, the intention to get gain
dishonestly, or to indulge in a pleasure that is
known to be unlawful, has got across the other good
intention.   This last intention is wholly bad.   Now,
looking at the case in this way, there is no intention
divided between the good and the evil, but there are
two distinct intentions, one wholly good, and one
wholly bad, trying to occupy the same mind at the
same time, like two straight lines trying to lie
between the same two points.   I do not believe
that this is possible ; therefore I do not think that
this is the correct way to represent these cases.   The
truth is that there is neither a mixed intention, nor
two distinct intentions, but one only.   There was a
good intention—the purpose to serve God truly and
acceptably.   This did exist in the mind, but in passing through the temptation, and in falling under
its power, another intention has become paramount,
and holds, for the time at least, complete control over
the mind.   That is, in the one case, the purpose to
gain money dishonestly, and in the other it is the
purpose to drink from some forbidden cup of pleasure.   When this last has gained the control of the
mind. the former good intention has been unconsciously let go.   The man may invent some subterfuge to satisfy himself that he has not let it go, but
it is gone, and the evil has come instead.   The most
that can be correctly said of his good intention at

the time of his committing the sin is that he hopes that sometime he will come again under that former good intention.

I therefore reach the conclusion that there can be but one ruling intention in a man's mind at the same time, and that this must be wholly good or wholly bad. I think that this is clearly taught in this text.

As to the effect upon a man's conduct of a change in the character of his intentions, there can be no doubt. It will make his acts appear like those of a man whose body is full of darkness. His conduct will be irregular. It will be like walking a rope with a swimming head. Let Blondin try to cross the Niagara river on his rope, and look down at the foaming waters, or around upon the wondering crowds of people, and he will fall.

A preacher from the country came into one of our western towns to preach. He had never spoken in so large a church, or to so great a company. As he stood in the high pulpit his head became dizzy. He did not fix his attention upon the book before him, or upon some point in the gallery, or better still, concentrate his thoughts upon his theme until he with eyes open would see nothing, but he allowed his eyes to wander about the room and to take in one after another of his hearers, until, as he afterwards said, the whole multitude seemed to be swimming around in the air. He had to close up his remarks abruptly, and get away. Now, that is just

what his conduct will be when a man gives up a
good intention for a bad one.   Here is one source of
weakness in our Christian work and influence.   We
not only indulge ourselves in coming down from
the strong intention to gain eternal life at all haz-
ards, and in frequently doing acts with a consciously
lower purpose, but we persuade ourselves that this
is unavoidable in our present state of being.   We
are therefore very lenient in our judgment of ourselves when we fall to acts with a very low intention.   Oh, we say, we cannot help it.   There is tremendous danger in this leniency.   Luther had this
danger in mind, when writing upon this same text.
He said it was a warning "not to allow ourselves to
be taken in by fair colors and outward appearance,
with which avarice may trick itself out and conceal
the knave."   But you may think that Luther was a
stern type of Christian man.   Yes, he was; but
nevertheless he was correct in this, that there is no
manner of excuse for any act which is done with a
bad intention.   It does not redeem the act in any
degree for the actor to say that he has a general intention in life to please God and gain eternal life,
because in saying that he either does not know his
own heart, or else he lies outright.   The good intention of a general character is dethroned when he
decides to do a single act with a bad purpose in his
heart.   Any amount of excuse may be made for the
act which was done with a good intention, but
which failed of its mark for want of more know-

ledge, or of a more steady hand, or of a better memory; but for an act with a bad design there is no apology now or ever.

I have spoken strongly on this subject; some of you may think I have spoken hard things. Well, I have felt willing to tear away that refuge which we are so likely to take, that we cannot avoid sometimes falling to a low purpose. I mentioned that preacher who said the congregation swam before his eyes. It was because he did not fix his attention in looking at the people. Well, I don't want you to swim before my eyes, either now or hereafter. I can look at you now without my head getting dizzy; but I could not do so by and by when we shall all stand in a much more solemn presence than this, if I did not try to hunt out the favorite hiding-places and subterfuges of the evil one who is daily robbing of all their bloom and fruitage Christian lives that were at their beginning full of hope and promise. We sit together here in the church to study the truth about motives and purposes. Let us also walk down into the city, let us stand together in market and store, and street and factory, in the office and at the polling-booth, in the kitchen and in the parlor, and there as well as here let us look after our Christian lives, and see that every individual act is informed by as earnest a desire to please God and to gain eternal life as we profess and feel in a general way when we sit in the congregation, or speak in the class-room. We can

reach a nobler standard of Christian living by dili-
gently attending to this matter.

Among other thoughts which insist upon being
noticed in this connection is the explanation which
this study gives of passages which represent that
men may live without sin. See, for example, 1 John
iii. 9; also 1 John v. 18. These mean that a man
when born of God comes under a new controlling influence. He is of God then, and he lives to Him
alone. As long as he keeps himself wholly under
that influence, he will not consent to do anything
which he knows that God will not approve. The
faults of his life through infirmity of body and
mind are not imputed to him as sin. They continue
until the end, but he will not be punished for them.
They do not prevent his enjoying the favor of God.

It is quite possible to attain to a condition of con-
secration in which we may enjoy the favor of God
without interruption. By living wholly in Christ
we shall be raised above any desire to do anything
that is not consistent with an earnest purpose to
gain eternal life. The strong intention to please
God may rule in every act.

Is not such a triumph of spiritual liberty worth
gaining?

A MAN IS ACCEPTABLE TO GOD IF HE MEANS TO DO RIGHT.

"If there be first a willing mind it is accepted according to that a man hath, and not according to that he hath not."— 2 CORINTHIANS viii. 12.

I INTENDED to preach a number of sermons encouraging a more earnest advance to higher attainments in the Christian life. My plan did not include anything upon the text which I have now read, but I turn to it that I may further explain some points already stated, and at the same time confirm the principles laid down.

The text was written to stimulate liberality in supporting an important charity. In such work the act is valued for the spirit that appears in it. If a man is poor he is not for that reason esteemed a small giver, if at the same time his soul is full of generous and helpful impulses. The gracious Lord said that the poor widow gave more than all the rest. She actually gave only two mites. They would not count for much in supporting the great work of the temple, or in feeding the hungry poor; but she so highly valued the privilege of giving something to the cause loved by God, that, looked upon in the spirit that prompted it, her gift was larger than any other.

Now, here is a principle enunciated which, I am sure, may be applied to all human conduct. If God will accept from a poor woman two two-ninths of one cent and count it as great a gift as another's thousands, then it is clear that He will make the same liberal allowance for a right state of mind in all other actions. With His judgment the condition of mind in which any act is done is the greatest part of the act.

Let it be the case of a sick person, confined to bed for many months, who longs to attend services for prayer and praise, to go through the streets on errands of mercy, carrying from cottage to cottage food for the hungry, and the bread of life for the soul; or let it be one to whom nature has given neither musical voice, nor sense of harmony, but who would delight to join actively in the high service of praise; or one who promised to go to the help of another, and sincerely intended to do so, but through pressure from many directions, forgot all about it; or let it be the case of a thoroughly honest man who wants to cast his vote in the right way, but who never had any opportunity of learning to read, and therefore cannot study up for himself the questions of the hour: now, is it not a reasonable interpretation of this text to say that God would in any of these cases accept the earnest desire to do the right thing, as if the act were actually done, when the failure has been due to some unavoidable defect of body or intellect ?

I think that this is the principle presented in this text, and I now desire to bring it to my aid in strengthening some principles that have been before laid down.

Beside a number of prayer-meeting talks, I have preached two sermons, bearing upon the higher gifts of grace. In the first I showed in what sense men in this life may become like Christ. It is only in the moral nature. This part of our humanity may realize in this world the full effect of Christ's redeeming work. To bring out my thought more clearly, I said that when one's moral nature is fully restored to its integrity he will not choose anything contrary to the will of God. He will intend, or mean, in everything he does, to do the right, and what is best to be done.

In the second sermon, I said that until life ends this same man will be engaged in perfecting holiness, which labor I said would be the teaching and disciplining of all his powers and faculties, that he may all the time be getting a little more nearly able to do just what he intends to do, though he will never quite accomplish this. There will always be some distance between what he wants to do, and what he does do.

Now, I want to work out my meaning until it is perfectly clear. So long as a teacher uses words which mean one thing to him, and something else

9

to his hearers, his meaning will not be well understood, because it is not clearly expressed. This is
just the way it has been in these sermons, between
you and me. I have been striving to discover,
through various conversations, just what meaning I
had conveyed, and after much thought, I think that
I have rooted out the difficulty.

It is this. In using the word "intention," I have
not meant what you have understood me to mean.
I think I can bring out the difference between us
on this point. There is an old saying, " Hell is
paved with good intentions." The authorship of
it is not known, but it is attributed to one of the
stern old divines. Now, when I am talking about
intentions, I think that you understand me to mean
about what is meant by the word in that saying.
When the old divine used that saying, I suppose
he meant a purpose that looks away into the
future for its fulfilment. Felix had such an intention when he said, " Go thy way for this time, when I
have a more convenient season I will call for thee."
I doubt not that he did intend sometime to send
for Paul, and attend to the grave matters in question. When the rich young man asked, " What
good thing shall I do to inherit eternal life ?" he had
an intention· which looked towards heaven, but
nevertheless he went away sorrowful. His intention did not bring forth any action. When young
men and women say, " I intend to die a Christian,"
and think that when they get settled in life, they

will then attend to these weighty questions, their
intention does not thrust up out of itself any deeds
that show a changed life. He intends to die a
Christian, yet goes on living in sin. It is much the
same with a drunkard, when he says to his wife
that he intends to reform his habits, and then goes
out and comes home drunk, and continues to do so
from time to time. So the gambler says, that when
he gains a hundred thousand dollars he intends to
quit the game, and to lead an honest life. Now, in
each of these cases there is an intention expressed,
which is followed by no action. It is a state of
mind which looks to the future for the realization
of some good that is deemed desirable. That is all
there is in such intentions. They amount simply to
an admission that it is desirable to get to heaven,
and that one cannot get there without being a
Christian here ; and therefore common sense dic-
tates that everyone should follow Christ.

These are the kind of good intentions with which
that severe old preacher said hell is paved.

If we would speak with philosophical accuracy,
they are not intentions at all, they do not inspire
any action. Actually the young man who says,
"I intend to be a Christian," and then goes away in
exactly the opposite direction, and continues to live
in sin, does not intend to be a Christian ; he
intends to live in sin, and so he does live. The
most he would say if he spoke correctly would be
that he hopes that sometime he will intend to
become a Christian, but that time is not yet.

Now, when I have been using the word "intention," you have been understanding me to mean such intentions as these with which hell is paved. Actually I have been meaning something entirely different. By intention I mean an essential part of every act. The moral philosophers tell us that there are four essential parts to every act. The first is the intention. To take a simple illustration, you are pleased with something your child has done. You think that she should have some reward. There is the first part of the act—the desire, the intention to reward your child. What shall you do for her ? The thought comes into your mind to give her a watch. That is the second part of the act. You may have thought of many ways of rewarding her, which you dropped, but this is the one you determine to carry out. The determination that you will do this, and not anything else, is the third part of the act. The fourth part anyone can see. You put on your hat and go to a jeweler's, and buy the watch, and bring it and place it in her hand. Three parts of an act are unseen by all but the actor, and God ; one alone is open to the eyes of all men. It is plain then that the intention is the very foundation of the act. It is the cause for which the act is done. It is a part of it, just as the edge is part of the knife, the point is part of a needle, or the box is part of a cart. It is that part of it for which all the rest exists, and without which all the rest would be quite useless.

Take that saying of the stern old divine, and translate it freely, hell is paved with the edges of knives, or with the points of needles. That would be absurd, because the edge of a knife, or the point of a needle is nothing at all when not on the knife or the needle. Take the edge away, and the whole knife is left, but it is utterly useless, because the end for which it was brought into existence is taken away. A knife was made to cut, and it cannot do this without an edge.

Now, whenever I have spoken about intentions I have always meant an intention which is a part of an action, not what a man has some kind of an idea that he will do sometime, but a part of the act which he is doing now. When I say if a man's moral nature is wholly restored he will always intend to do what is right, I do not mean that he will have a general intention to do right in life, but that in every separate act which he does he will have a definite intention to do right in that particular.

He can afford a separate intention for each act of his life. Not like the man who prayed by looking at his written prayer and saying, " thems my sentiments," he has not to refer back to his intentions when he first made a profession of religion, but under each act he has a distinct intention, and that intention is good. I do not mean that in the case of each act he stops to think out that particular case, for he intends well without stopping to analyze his feeling. If, however, an evil purpose were thrust upon him he would feel that. An educated man speaks correctly all day without thinking of any rule of grammar, but any marked error in speech would cause him to think of the rules of grammar.

Now, if I have been successful in making my meaning plain, we are ready to apply the principle contained in the text to these cases where one's performance is not so good as it was intended to be.

There is an appeal for gifts to carry on a certain charity. A man feels in his heart that he would like to endow it with a hundred thousand dollars, but he is a poor man, and from the wages paid for his daily toil, he gives only ten dollars, but it is half his earnings for a month. To give so much he has stinted himself in the matter of necessary food, to say nothing about going without all useless indulgences. Now, does not this text teach that God would esteem him a liberal giver? Would not you also say that he was more liberal than many who gave twenty times the amount he gave? You also would esteem his act in the light of his intention, or for the spirit which it manifested.

Let us see how this principle will apply to other things. You send your little girl, say ten years old, into the town, on a message that it is important to you to have delivered immediately. To avoid a group of drunken, swearing men, which you did not take into your calculation, she turns aside from the direct route which you instructed her to take. The result is that she gets lost, and after wandering about for many hours, she at last returns, without delivering her message, when it is too late to be of any advantage to you to have it delivered.

Now, the execution of her act has been bad, and the result is vexatious to you, as well as being the cause of considerable loss. What will you do with your little girl? Will you fall upon her with a severe beating? If you do you are a brute, and deserve worse than a beating yourself. But that is the very last thing that you will think of. You feel that the child is as innocent as an angel. Because of her intention, and her honest effort to serve you, you feel as kindly toward her as if she had actually accomplished all you desired. There was a willing mind, and you accept the act as if perfectly done, because according to her ability she did the best she could. A strong man might have done it better, but she was not a strong man. The part of her act which we call the intention was perfect.

Take this principle into any sphere, and it will work the same way. Your grocer leaves your order at the wrong door. It is awkward, indeed, for you. You have some friends in to tea. At last you send around to him again. He apologizes and is extremely mortified, and neglects everything else in his effort to remedy the mistake. It is all due to an ignorant boy who cannot read numbers with any

confidence that he is correct. What will you do
about it ? Will you abandon your grocer ? No,
you come in the end to pity him, and to feel that he
suffers more from the affair than you do. Will you
insist that he dismiss that boy ? No, for he is a
useful boy, he is naturally bright, and is learning
the numbers fast, and it would be cruel to cut off
his living when he is doing his best, and that best
is fairly well.

In all these cases you would accept the deed as if
it were well done, because the person tried his best
to do it well. He failed through some imperfection
of hand or memory or judgment. Well now, that
is God's way of dealing with us. When the heart
means well He accepts the imperfect performance of
an act as though it were perfect, that is, He makes
allowance for the poor ability we have with which
to perform a perfect act, or to carry out a perfect
intention.

Well now, through this opening, I think that we
can see the true relation which a wholly saved man
sustains to both God and men.

First, as to God. He lives in Christ, and honestly
wants to do what Christ would have him do in
each separate act of his life. There is something
more than a general intention to live a Christian
life. That intention comes down into everything he
does. If he has not such an intention in every act,
he is not living in Christ at all. The moment he
enters upon one act without the desire and intention

to do what will please God in that act, he has departed from God, and is committing a sin. Seeing that he intends to do the will of God in all things, though his performance is far from perfect, God accepts it as perfect, " according to what he hath, and not according to what he hath not." That is, God takes into the account the implements with which he has to work, and so, as long as he means what is right, the imperfect execution is freely forgiven and overlooked.

Second, as to men. It is plain that to men the same holy man's life must appear defective. He has to carry out all his good plans and purposes with most imperfect instruments. The body and mind will constantly betray him into error. Take the old fable of the birds. In that story the crow intended to sing as well as the lark, but for want of voice, and sense of harmony, and everything else that enters into the nature of music, the crow's attempt was a distinguished failure. So a good many good intentions come out in the execution. And so it will be with every man, until the end of his life. The best man living or who ever did, or ever will live, must feel that his efforts fall far short of what he meant and desired them to be. He is every day trying to correct the defects of the past, but probably every day feeling more than ever the utter hopelessness of ever reaching perfection in his performance.

Now, he will often be blamed for these imperfec-

tions by men. Men cannot forgive as easily as God
can, and they are more exacting than He, because
they know less. Men can only know of each
other's intention by what each succeeds in accomplishing; consequently they cannot make the same
allowance which God does for a poor performance,
because of the good intention which lies behind it.
They cannot see the good intention. Then it is also
true that God understands better than men what
each one has to work with, for men differ so much
in their endowments, and each is likely to make
his own endowments and attainments the judgment
bar at which he wants every other man to be tried.

Men's uncharitableness, their treatment of each
other in this respect, is nothing less than cruel.
There is a man who has a vigorous body, a naturally
bright intellect, thoroughly developed by a university training, and who never knew what it means to
feel shame on account of any of his kindred. His
business has always been prosperous. His high
gifts have enabled him to make it so. He has
never felt any of the privations of poverty. Now,
it is an easy thing to that man to be self-possessed,
to be calm, and to be thoroughly moral. He criti-
cises, and ridicules, and heaps his contempt upon
plain men who, without a tithe of his advantages,
and with tools immeasurably inferior to his, are
trying to render a good account of themselves in
this world, to walk uprightly and to enter heaven
at last.

This is only one example of many hard judgments which men form of each other's conduct. Men can hardly understand why every other should not do as well in any case as the man who happens to sit in judgment at any moment on any particular action. They do not readily take into account the difference in each other's endowments and educational advantages.

1. From this study we may learn what is meant when the epistles of John teach that if a man is born of God he will not commit sin. He will not intend to offend God.

2. It should teach us the principle upon which we should exercise a universal charity. About the least allowance we can make for any man is that he may be in the favor of God, and if he should die he would get into heaven. That is no great praise for any man. It is all of God's boundless grace.

3. It also teaches us wherein our true excellency lies. The man who turns his talent to account will get a reward. To do this he must make all his faculties serve his pure intention with something like efficiency. Herein is a work for which he is worthy of praise.

4. It also affords a basis for the distribution of rewards and punishments.

ONE GRAVE DEFECT.

" Yet lackest thou one thing."—LUKE xviii. 22.

ONE thing indeed! If I lacked no more than that, I should think it scarcely worth mentioning.

Of five thoughts suggested by this text, the first is:

I. That a person who lacks only one thing should be counted a very happy person. Why, he was happy that he did not lack twenty things. It would require a caravan to carry the things that almost anyone imagines he wants. How easily wants grow in our minds! How rapidly the formidable list accumulates! But we can dispense with most of these things without any inconvenience. Often we are better without than with them. If a man can give himself and his family three meals each day, clothe them respectably, and educate his children, we shall not stop to pity him because he cannot afford a carriage and pair, or because his wife frets because her carpets cost twenty-five cents per yard less than her neighbor's. If the silly creature cannot stand that, she gets no sympathy from me.

But there is a strange fascination about a person who can have all he wants. Trollope, in "The Small House at Allington," represents an English girl as wondering if a bishop ever has his gloves stitched when they break out at the seams. With her stitching, and pressing, and mending, her ideal of happiness was one who never needed to do anything of the kind.

We stand before mansions and imagine the life of the people within them—people who never need to say, "I can't," for want of money. No darning and scrimping. Some of them do not lack anything. But then some of them may lack many things, as health, beauty, love, innocence. Often the owner would give all for the health his coachman enjoys. The mistress would give up her place in life for the beauty of her maid, or if her husband would love her as her gardener loves his wife.

And worst of all is the lack of innocence. The money that built the mansion was gained by fraud. The owner sleeps, and a nightmare seizes him. He hears ever the crying of the orphans whose father he ruined, and who died of a broken heart. Oh, will no one stop the crying of those children! We do not know as we stand before mansions, but all the same if we did know that anyone lacked only one thing, we should count him very happy !

A second thought that crowds along, is :

II. If a man lacked but one thing, that thing might be something the absence of which would prevent his getting any good from all that he possessed. The boy uttered a typical truth who said, "Salt was what made potatoes taste bad by not having any on." The idea is, the loss of what you have because you have not something else. In your watch is a small spring, so small, indeed, that you would scarcely see it on your table. It is the hair spring. But it is so important that, lacking it, your watch would be utterly useless. The heavy case of gold, the elaborately wrought machinery, the fitness of all the other parts, would be of no value. It is only one thing, but that thing is essential.

A palace, with all that money can bring by way of furnishings, and even royal equipage, but the mistress is blind! A table loaded with all delicacies and luxuries, but the man is ill and cannot eat!

I visited a young man twenty years of age, wealthy and popular, belonging to a good family. He had only a short time before fallen heir to a handsome fortune. He had been, when in health, a person of very fine appearance. Everything that heart could wish for was at that man's command. But there was one defect—his health was gone. He was far gone in consumption. It was plain that there were not many more days for him upon earth. As we talked, he wept bitterly. "Oh," he exclaimed, "to be cut off in my prime! It is very hard." To me it was a sad spectacle. If there had been fewer attractions to his lot, his distress would not have been so great.

This is true in every case where a person has no religion. He does not get the highest good of anything in life because of lacking this one thing in life. Does he say he gets the good of life as he goes along? Then he puts himself on the level of a child eating a stick of candy. Now, if there were any way in which a child could eat the candy and have it, would he not seek that way? There is not; when he eats it, it is gone forever, and if it were a mile long it would soon be gone. So, without religion, there is nothing left of life when one has passed through it. There is a way by which he can have it and yet keep every part of it, but he does not follow that way, and so loses it as he uses it. But he accumulates as he goes along! Yes, we used to roll snowballs. "Hark! the school bell! Oh, boys, what a ball we could make if the noon hour lasted till sundown! But we have to go into school. We cannot take it home at night. It can only melt away where it lies." So with man's accumulations. But with religion he carries his past forward with him in the virtues of his own character. But without it, as he gets near the end he learns that he has lived in vain, under a painted heaven, with beads for stars. Lacking religion, he loses the good of all that he ever possesses.

But yet another thought about lacking only one thing.

III. The one thing lacking may be some essential thing.

On the 30th day of January, 1649, the physical
manhood of Charles I. lacked only one thing, but
that thing was his head. It was the defect of an
essential thing.

I said just now I would give no sympathy to the
person who wanted a carriage or better carpets; but
if one of the children is sick, and we know some
particular thing that will give that child relief, we
will walk around the city to procure it, and bring it
to the child. So if this man mentioned here lacks
some thing essential to life and happiness, we are
bound to give the case our most serious consideration. Why, just think, leaving that one thing un-
supplied might prove fatal.

Yea, it is possible that lacking some one thing
might shut the gates of heaven against him; might
blot his name out of the book of life. To lack one
essential thing is a matter of very grave importance.
It is a case not to be classed among those in which
men accumulate imaginary wants.

But let us turn again to the case of this man.
Perhaps the one thing he lacked was some essential thing. In that case we must not pass him by
with a sneer.

Now, this can very easily be the case in relation
to religion. There is one essential thing here. It is
conformity to Christ. That includes three things:
1. Trust in His atonement for the forgiveness of all
sin; 2. Likeness to His spirit, or inward life in Him;
and 3. Imitation of His example in outward life.

The first two of these, and more especially the *first*, are liable to be overlooked. A man may be in many respects like a Christian, but if he lacks the spirit of Christ, if he has no personal dependence upon Him, then assuredly all the good that he has will be lost, so far as getting him into heaven is concerned.

And yet a fourth thought crowds upon us here:

IV. When only one thing is lacking a person is less likely to discover his need of it than if he lacked many things.

He will have so much that is good that his eye will be filled with it, and he will probably not discover that one thing is still wanting. Now, you can easily bring together in your thoughts a multitude of things which a man may have and yet be lacking to the extent of one thing.

Mrs. —— bought $1,100 worth of goods of J—— A——, in an hour. A month later she saw "fairy lights," and must have some. He told her she got some when in before. She had never unpacked them, but had so much she never missed them.

Now construct an ideal Christian.

(*a*) There may be, to begin with, an amiable temper, good health, a happy adjustment of mental qualities, a manner of life largely free from the causes that stir up the sterner qualities of human nature. Let all these conditions meet in one person and he will be amiable in his temper and outward manner. You may remember Becky Sharpe's criti-

10

cism of the mistress of Queen's Crawle, a woman
who had been beautiful, but was beautiful no longer.
Her eyes seemed always ready to fill with tears as
if weeping the loss of her departed charms. She
had been so systematically trampled upon by Sir
Pitt, and so systematically ignored by everyone
else that no spirit was left in her. Becky shrewdly
reflected, " I have nothing to fear from that woman."
Now that is one type of amiability. How unlikely
such a person is to find out that, as a Christian, he
lacks anything! Yet such gentleness is not religion! The soft, gentle meekness, which is simply
the absence of any true force of character, may be
present and yet one thing, or more, be lacking.
Why, this young man had all this softness and
attractiveness of character. We are told that Jesus
loved him. What does this mean but that his dis-
position was so gentle that Jesus was won by it?
But it was not religion. It is unworthy the name,
however. But when there are fire, and passion, and
energy, all held under restraint, so that one does
not speak or look the savage word that burns within,
and with almost volcanic power seeks utterance,
there is true amiability. But a person must have
some of the spirit of Christ to restrain himself in
that way.

(b) One may also have had a religious training in
childhood. Suppose that from your earliest years
you had scrupulously observed all the commandments, you would, undoubtedly, also have followed

the habits of pious people. In that case you would
be no better than this young man. His answers to
the Saviour reveal the fact that his parents had
been scrupulously careful to lead his steps in his
youth into the ways of religion.

(c) As a result of this religious training in childhood and youth, he had a high degree of religious
knowledge. But knowledge of subjects related to
religion is a very different thing from personal piety.
An infidel may seek this knowledge. An intelligent
Chinaman, one of the higher class, was travelling on
an American railway. He was engaged in conversation with an American gentleman of good intelligence. The discussion was about Christianity.
The Chinaman was much interested. He put many
pertinent questions, and showed a great interest in
the progress of the Christian religion, and its influence and teaching. The American thought him
about to embrace it. With a few adroit sentences,
he gave the conversation a personal turn. But now
to his amazement the Chinaman declared that China
had the best system of religion in the world. He
said that it was much more likely that the religion
of China would prevail over all the rest of the
world than that Christianity would ever prevail to
any great extent in China. Now, he was seeking a
knowledge of Christian religion just as a boy studying English history enquires about the Lollards or
Druids. He had no idea of becoming a Druid or a
Lollard. So this Chinaman sought the knowledge

of this religion just as the late Prof. Agassiz used to
seek a knowledge about snakes, often storing them
away, greatly to his convenience, in his wife's slip-
pers, and thus furnishing the good woman some
great surprises. Such enquiries about religion are
just like a boy's enquiries about a menagerie. He
has no intention of buying it. If he had, his enquiries would be of a very different nature. A
man may have any amount of knowledge about
religion, acquired in this way, and yet lack all conformity to Christ. But when he seeks knowledge
as Zaccheus did, wanting it to apply to his own
heart and life, he will become like that man, ready
to sacrifice and do anything.

Now, take any one, or two, or three, or four of
these qualifications of the ideal Christian—how
unlikely he who has them is to discover that anything is lacking to his Christian character! More
if you add—

(d) Regular and habitual reading of the Bible.
There is such a thing as using the Bible as a sort of
atonement for past sin and neglect. It is not
necessarily religious. Reading the Bible as a sort
of religious task is very different from incorporating
the spirit of the Bible into one's heart. I remember a man who every day of his life contradicted
the spirit of the Bible, but who seemed to think
that the reading of a few chapters on the Sabbath
was a sufficient offset to all his irreligion during the
week. Another had neglected religion all his life,

but when he found himself near the end of life, he said, " Bring me the Bible, I must now read it and get ready to die." Now, it is the getting the spirit of the Bible into our hearts, and revealing it in our lives that makes a man ready to die, and not simply running the eye over the words it contains. The fact is that the Bible was not given particularly to teach men how to die. It was designed to teach men how to live, and it is wholly incidental that it teaches us how to die. If one learns from it how to live well, there need be no concern about the dying. That will come out all right. If this use has not been made of the book while living, then nothing that can be done in the extreme moment will avail anything. The case will then have gone out of our hands. It will have been delivered to the jury. The book long ours, long wholly in our hands, will then have passed into the possession of the court as matter of evidence. It will be ours no longer.

What chance has the regular Bible reader to dis-cover that his religious character and life lack any-thing? Especially when he makes a virtue of his regular habit !

(e) Membership in the Church. A man may also be a member of the Church of Christ and yet be wanting in some essential thing. Certainly this young man was a member of the established Church of his time. Indeed, he filled a very high position in the Church. We are told that he was a

ruler. He was not a civil ruler, but an ecclesiastical ruler. Yet he was not thoroughly supplied
for the change that awaited him. There is a saying
which originated in no good will, in times of great
religious degeneracy, the truth of which under certain circumstances is often yet strikingly illustrated.
It is. "The nearer to the Church, the farther from
God." This seems to have been the case with this
young man. It is painfully true of many who
regularly attend the services of religion. It is not
the Church, but Christ, that saves.

A man may be morally correct in his life and yet
be wanting in some essential thing. If a man obeys
the commandments he must be a moral man. Hence
this youth was not wanting in this. Morality is no
guide as to whether a man has the spirit which God
requires in him. If morality springs from a person's spirit, it will be a perfect exhibition that he is
or is not what God would have him be, and
especially in this age when there are so many other
causes that produce morality. What is called society
demands from a person so high a degree of rectitude
that to be countenanced by decent people a man
must in outward life appear to be as good as a
Christian. You may say, in the case of any
moral man, that you do not know whether he is
moral because he loves purity or because he respects
the feelings and opinions of his fellowmen. You
may say it is none of our business to know. This
is true. But it is his business to know if he is think-

ing himself fit for heaven because he is moral. That is the whole point we make here.

Again, the circumstances of some men's lives make morality much more easy to them than to others. There is as much difference between men in this respect as there is between the green bough which waves in beauty upon the tree, and the white ashes which lie upon the hearth. The one has had the bright sunshine and the refreshing dew, the other has been cut off and passed through the fire. The ashes had been still green leaves had the circumstances remained the same. So in life. There sits a judge upon the bench, and before him is a prisoner at the bar. They represent the two extremes in relation to the law. The one is the law honored, the other is the law broken. The one is perfect morality, the other is immorality. But now consider the different circumstances through which these two men have come in life. The one was the child of respectable parents. They always gave him enough of life's necessaries. In his childhood he never felt the pinching fingers of want upon him. Why should he be tempted to steal? In childhood and youth he always saw an example of integrity and propriety before him. Under such circumstances how easy it was for him to turn aside from all vicious and depraved ways. Well educated, when he reached manhood he was launched by the position and influence of others upon an honorable and high career. He never once wrestled with the crimes that brought the criminal before him to the bar. But that criminal has come, we will suppose, through a very different course. He was born in poverty and misery. No one ever took him by the hand to lead him to church or to school. His struggles with evil and misfortune began in the cradle, and they have been renewed every day of his life. He came upon crime as a birthright. Perhaps if the circumstances of these two men had been reversed they might have also exchanged positions. This is of course only an imaginary case. It is by no means universal. On the contrary, some of the best men have come up through just such straits as this criminal. But this hypothetical case represents how easily some men may have a correct morality, while others, always striving with mighty resistance against evil, still show a life outwardly defective. To get the true value of morality as it must appear weighed by God's standard, we should know how much has been resisted in each case. As compared with each other, one man has to run an engine that could draw the longest train America ever saw over the Rocky Mountains; another has but to guide a baby's carriage. The one has to keep in accord with the voices around him a trumpet which could be heard from Nova Zembla to Cape Horn ; another has but to guide the mellow tones of a flute through the rising chorus. Surely God has some way by which these two men stand upon a common level as regards salvation. In judging a man's morality we should know how much comes from a true love of goodness, and how much from the fear of society.

Now, here are three, yea, five, valuable things which we have brought together. There is good temper, religious training in childhood, much religious knowledge, membership with the Church, and an unobjectionable morality. We might specify farther. Now, with such wealth of good qualities united in one's character, would it not be difficult to persuade himself that he could possibly be lost ? Could he easily fix his attention upon the fact that one essential thing was wanting in him ? The very excellence of his character would make it harder to discern that he is wanting in the one thing—conformity to Christ ?

When you go down among vile men you may reproach them in strong terms, for they know that they are sinners. You may charge their immorality upon them and they will feel it every time. If a man never goes to church you have some chance with him, but when there is everything that a person needs except one, it is very difficult to bring home to him the truth that he is in danger because of some one defect. If a number of points were defective, there would be no difficulty in the case. But we must not deceive ourselves. Some things are of essential value. We need all other virtues and graces, but we cannot possibly get along without this. A general reproved an officer under him for some defective conduct. The officer said it would not occur again. " Ah," said the general, " in the army there is no room for a second miscarriage." So, concerning that test to which we are all looking, there is no room for a second miscarriage. If we miss once there will be no opportunity for a second attempt.

V. And now we come upon a fifth thought suggested by lacking only one thing.

If one fails who lacked only one thing, the fact that he lacked so little only aggravates the disappointment of his failure.

A student failing in his examination by just a few marks in only one subject—how vexatious! Twenty-two years ago this month, Gen. Grant led his victorious army into Vicksburg. A painful tragedy occurred as the rejoicing soldiers went shouting into the prostrated city. A private soldier caught up a rifle, which the enemy had thrown down, and holding it by the muzzle, he dragged it after him as he rushed forward, and the hammer caught upon the ground, the gun was discharged, the bullet passing through the man's body, and killing him instantly. What a sad death! The young man had passed without harm through several hard-fought battles ; he had escaped sickness in hard marches, and during the siege ; he would now go into garrison with his comrades, and be safe for the rest of the war. He was within a step of home and friends. The welcome home, the paternal blessing, the greeting of his old friends were near. He lacked, oh, so little, yet that reunion could never be. All the joy of victory, all the applause of the nation, all the honors and rewards of duty well done, all the chance of promotion, all, all were lost because he lacked one thing. There is a proverb which soldiers use when they learn that a bullet has gone through their hat. It is this, "A miss is as good as a mile." It is a somewhat dangerous proverb, because it is likely to make us forget the calamity when the miss is on the other side. When we miss getting any good thing, then a miss is as bad as a mile. To just miss some promotion is to be left to the monotony of our old paths. To miss heaven, though by but the narrowest chance, is as bad as an eternity of misfortune. I think that this side of the oft-quoted proverb is of much more consequence than the other.

In the Bible or out of it, I know of no sadder case than that of this young man. There was much to make life in this world attractive to him. He was a well-to-do person. He was young. Already he had risen to some distinction. He was a ruler. He had all that wealth could bring. His family was popular. He shared in the general esteem. What young man would not exchange lot for lot with him. Two of the evangelists tell of his coming to Jesus. The great Teacher dealt with him in such a faithful way as he had never been accustomed to before. Jesus held him up before his eye. He looked through

his very soul. He told him just what he needed,
and how it was to be obtained. The lesson seemed
to him to be a hard one to put into practice. He
turned away sorrowful. There is no syllable or
sign to indicate that he ever performed the duty
pointed out to him. The last we see of him his
face has turned fully toward the world and his back
upon heaven. It is an attitude full of no promise
for his future. Oh, it was a sad ending for a course
which opened full of hopeful inquiry.

Just a word as to the one thing which he lacked.
I have said it was conformity to Christ, including a
trust in His work for salvation, the possession of
Christ's spirit in himself, and the imitation of His
example. Now, how do the instructions which
Jesus gave to him justify that statement ? Why,
just in this way : Jesus instructed him in substance
to get the world out of his heart. Sell all that thou
hast and give the proceeds to the poor. If he could
do that there would be no danger of his being
destroyed or injured by the love of the world.
Now, this meant, in a word, that the love of the
world prevented his full acceptance of Jesus. The
love of the world prevented his full conformity to
Christ.

We cannot study this young man's case without
having our thoughts turned to the ending of our
own earthly course. It is easy to have religion
enough to get well through this world, but the question crowds upon us, " will that be sufficient to get

us well through the last trying ordeal?" The saddest possible thought of such an hour is the contrast between what we shall be at that hour and what we were, and what we hoped and promised ourselves that we should be, and what we might have been, and what we ought to have been, and what we would have been but for ourselves. Some time since some miners brought up from a deep mine the body of a poor fellow who, more than forty years before, had been suffocated in the mine. Some chemical agent had come in contact with the body, and it had been preserved through all the long period as fresh as it was on the day when the accident occurred. There he lay at the mouth of the pit, a ruddy young man, his black locks falling back from his brow, and his face the picture of health as it was on that sad day forty years before. No one recognized him. A whole generation had passed away since the last time he descended the shaft to engage in his daily toil. By and by an old woman came up more than sixty years old. She knew him in a moment, for during all those long years he had not been forgotten for a single day. He was to have become her husband on the day after that on which the accident occurred. The bent, wrinkled, gray, old woman fell upon the form of the young man, and poured into his deaf ear words of endearment such as she had not spoken for forty years. There was a strange contrast between the two, and yet they belonged to each other, both as to betrothal and as to time. Only in the two one saw by contrast the change which time is constantly making in us all. He had remained unchanged; she had grown old.

Now, in those two I see a picture of the change which time is making with us all, in our moral natures, as well as in our bodies. At seventy we differ as much from what we were at twenty-five as that gray, worn, old woman differed from the form of her affianced as he was at twenty-five. But none of us intended that time should change our moral natures so much. We hoped and planned to preserve our purity without blemish.

There is one way, and only one, whereby we may keep our moral natures as fresh and pure and simple as we were at twenty, or even at ten, that is, by enshrining the love of Christ in our hearts. Conformity to Him, if we make it the first aim of our lives, will save us from all depreciation.

RELIGIOUS CAPACITY LOST BY NEGLECT.

" For unto every one that hath shall be given, and he shall have abundance ; but from him that hath not shall be taken away even that which he hath."—MATTHEW xxv. 29.

THIS text states a general law, observed everywhere in life and in nature. In a few words the law may be stated as simply loss by neglect, and increase by use. Everyone has made some observations which uphold this law, but the most startling results from its operation are seen in relation to a man's capacity for religion. If this capacity is used, it grows strong and full of healthful energy, but if it is neglected it perishes entirely. This is in substance the meaning of this parable of the talents, for in a strictly critical interpretation of it, its principles must be applied to man's religious nature. Certainly there can be no objection, in a general way, to make the talent represent any power to influence others, as for example, grace or beauty of person, strength and power of endurance, or any intellectual gifts, such as those which make a man proficient in learning, in trade or art.

But at the present time we shall take the more critical view of the parable, and engage our thoughts

wholly upon what may be called the religious
talents. By these I do not mean talents which may
be used in connection with religion. This may be
done with every endowment of bodily strength, and
with all the faculties of the intellect. They may all
be used in the service of religion; indeed, a truly
religious man does constantly press them into the
service of his God. Herein they reach their highest
aim. But by the religious talents I mean those
which can be used only in connection with religion.
They are wholly idle and neglected in an irreligious
man.

I have met the true statement that the greatness
of a creature may be measured by the wants it manifests. Take, for example, a stone. It wants only a
place in which to lie. A tree also wants a spot in
which to stand, but that is not all. It must constantly draw upon the exhaustless treasures of the
many-bearing earth, it must bathe its waving arms
in the wealth of the sun's light. How much grander
the existence of a tree than that of a stone. But a
bird rises to a yet grander height than either. It
must be allowed to soar through the limitless heavens,
and to feed upon the developed fruits of the earth,
and unconsciously it taxes daily a magnificent Providence as its great housekeeper. But much higher
than the bird do some animals rise in the scale of
being, measured by their wants. They need all that
I have mentioned as demanded by these other creatures, and more, even to a sort of kindred or fellow-

ship with man. This is a curious and interesting phase of animal life. Certainly on the lower plane of their existence they are like man. I do not know of any difference between my animal life, and the animal life of a horse which I may drive. But, you say, my life is my soul. Without it my body is dead, and at once begins to decay. Yes, but I will say that the horse certainly has also a soul, so far as a soul is necessary to animal life. The Greeks and the Romans described the animal life of the beast and that of a man by the same words. It was the same word which they used for the soul of a man. And they were right, so far as it is reasonable to say that a beast has a soul, but not so highly endowed as the soul of man. It has all the power that a man's soul has to keep the body alive. In this respect it is as good a soul as any of us have, but it is wanting in all the endowments which make human existence so grand and glorious. There can be no reasonable objection to calling this animal endowment a soul. All language is to serve us, and the word soul must serve like all other words. If it be complained that it makes the word convey an indefinite meaning, I answer that the souls of men are far from being equal in power. Then there is likeness with diversity between man and animals in every part of their being. Their bodies have organs which may be nourished by the same food, but they cannot be taught to do the same things. The limbs of an animal are not as susceptible to

11

education as those of a man. Why then should the beast not have a soul also less susceptible to instruction and elevation ? Some animals can enter in some small degree into fellowship with man. They can reach up just to the lowest side of his nature. That is all. But the human soul is so nobly endowed that man reaches up through all the stages of a developing ambition, through the conquest of kingdoms, through the triumph over the material universe, through all the secrets of nature, and the high and divine mysteries of knowledge, until at last the higher side of his nature reaches away into the heavens, and finds its highest goal in fellowship with God, just as the noblest animals begin to have fellowship with the nature of man. In God man lives, moves and has his being. There is something wrong and unnatural in any man who feels in himself no want of God. I know that through the misfortune of human sin men fail to recognize this want. Until awakened to the high aims for which their nature was created, they are like a tree which stands in its little plot of ground, and is all unconscious that it is every moment feeding upon the affluent air, and drawing from the exhaustless treasures of the patient earth. It thinks it is all contained in itself. So are many men. They live upon God and know it not. They deny Him, and yet He is the constant spring of their existence.

1. I begin with the soul's hunger for God. That the human soul, in its normal state, does hunger for

God is as true as that the body needs food. It is as
natural as for a woman to crave affection. It is
simply the child nature in man, which never is entirely lost from him, craving and crying out for its
father. The infant's clinging to his father is but
the babyhood of the human desire for God. The
infant loves and obeys and depends with sweet, im-
plicit confidence upon his parent; but with passing
years all this feeling of dependence is outgrown.
The father is the same to him as another man,
except in the affection which survives because of
the tender and precious associations of the past.
The fact is that the infant has transferred to God, in
every natural and proper case, all the feelings
which during infancy it bestowed upon the human
father. I say in every natural and proper case,
because it is agreeable to the nature given to us to
grow up into God. God is the first, the last, and
the supreme want of the human soul.

Here we see the high glory of our being. A stone
can know nothing. Some vegetables have a slight
perception of touch. They can feel what produces
no impression upon a stone. But the higher orders
of animals all have the five senses in a high degree
of development. Some of them seem to possess the
power of purely intellectual operations, to some
small degree, at least as much as is involved in acts
of memory and association.

But man leaps at one stroke immeasurably
beyond all these achievements, and dashes on in pur-

suit of all knowledge. He boldly connects fact
with fact, and so builds up a grand structure of
reasoning. He places his foot upon a simple known
truth which lies upon the surface of the earth as it
were, and the last conclusion in his argument
touches the distant skies. He sends his thought
down through the mysteries of nature. The scientific man's insight into nature amounts almost to
prophecy. But this power is not the highest faculty
of knowledge possessed by him; it is not the faculty
of which I am speaking. Incalculably higher than
this is the faculty by which man knows God. It is
not the ability to rise by induction from nature up
to nature's God, to reach the reasonable conclusion
that the visible universe had a maker, and that
maker is God, to follow the winding path of infer-
ence until at last it triumphantly lands him at the
Godhead—not that alone is man's highest faculty of
knowledge, but from within himself is opened a
window directly upon the Deity, and through it
pours down from God upon the soul a revelation, as
it were, of the existence of God, and in some
measure of His character. In this way a man becomes as confident of the existence of God as he is
of his own existence. " And hereby we do know
that we know Him."

2. Another religious talent is man's ability to be
impressed, enlightened, influenced, guided and led
by the Spirit of God. " As many as are led by the
Spirit of God." " He will guide you into all truth."

"He shall receive of mine, and shall show it unto you." Now, this capacity is peculiar to man. But, you ask, may not the Divine Spirit work through any medium? Why, yes, the Spirit once used chaos, out of which to make a world. The Spirit once used the ass, which Balaam rode, to reprove a guilty man. And so He may do at any time; but these were miraculous manifestations of the divine power. The point is, that when the Spirit speaks to and through man's heart, it is no miracle at all, but is simply the natural way of doing this work. Man's nature was made to be dealt with in this manner. He has a faculty through which it can be accomplished, and it is man's normal condition to receive communications from God in this way. The Spirit of God could not speak through a book, or a block of wood, without first working a miracle, and endowing the book or block with power or faculty to receive such a communication. But, in man's case no miracle is necessary, for he has the faculty already. It was through this faculty that inspiration came upon men. This was only a higher and fuller degree of communication. Man is yet capable of receiving knowledge by inspiration. Now, what a crowning distinction of man is this! There is nothing like it in any creatures of which we have any positive knowledge. The more intelligent animals give us a faint idea of this high quality in human nature. "The sheep know the shepherd's voice, and a stranger will they not follow, but will flee from him, for they know not the voice of strangers."—John x. 45. They know the voice of their master. They submit to the guidance of that voice. This is the highest to which they can rise. But man rises into a capacity to be guided directly by God Himself.

3. Yet another distinct religious talent is the capacity to feel a sense of obligation to God. This will appear to be a distinctly marked faculty of the human soul, if you will take the trouble to understand just what obligation to God is. It is not the obligation which a man feels when he has been served with a writ, and then for the first time says that he "ought" to pay that debt; or what another feels when he is violating the law and sees a policeman coming, and then he says, "I ought to get away from here"; or what one feels when guilty of a flagrant theft, and then he says, "I ought to cross the national boundary." There are many examples of men using "I ought" in such a sense as that. A dog might speak with as high a sense of obligation. He is robbing the kitchen and sees the owner approach, and he says, "I ought to get out from here," and forthwith he sets to work to get out. Now, the "I ought" of a man must be of more binding obligation than the "I ought" of a beast, or it is unworthy the name of obligation at all. When I speak of that endowment whereby man has the ability to say "I ought," I mean that he can feel in the highest sense his obligation as unto God. I mean

the sense of obligation which bends the weary toiler under his heavy task for love's dear sake. I mean that sense of obligation which leads the traveller over stormy seas, and bleak barren mountains, until at last upon his long-strained eyes there bursts again the loved sight of home. I mean the sense of obligation which carries the soldier over bloody fields and sends him home at last with an empty sleeve, or a wooden leg, or stretches him out to die on the plain, under the blazing stars, his last thought being of the loved home he shall never see again, and his last prayer for the loved ones whom he has sacrificed for his country, or that those who live in coming ages may be free. I mean the "I ought" which carries the missionary, with wife and children, away from the home of their early years to spend their lives amid scenes of savagery, and under the rank superstitions and gross domestic customs of heathen peoples. I mean the "I ought" which tears the martyr from a mansion of splendor, from wealth and ease, and from holy love, and leads him up to the stake or the gibbet to die without a murmur. It is the "I ought" which carries Jesus through Gethsemane, and up to Calvary, and makes even the despised cross a better thing than shame and a denial of the truth.

Such a sense of obligation as this is like the step of the Almighty in the human soul. It is as solemn and weighty and awful as the walking of the Almighty in the garden at evening time.

Now, this is a separate religious faculty. It is not merely a conviction that arises in the mind from reasoning about the relative value of good and evil, of wisdom and folly, of truth and righteousness. It is a divine gift, a distinct endowment of man's nature, bestowed upon him in his creation. It is a capacity possessed by no other creature of which we have knowledge.

4. Yet another, and the last of these religious faculties which I will mention now is faith. I mean faith in God. There is faith everywhere. In the world of business it is omnipotent. In social life it is the foundation of all happiness. But I mean a distinct faith which has God for its object. This is to religion what experiment is in natural science. For example, a philosopher has certain theories about light. But he knows nothing truly as yet. However, he begins to experiment. It is Newton. He failed to prove what he desired to prove about light because his experiments were at fault. He allowed the light to enter a darkened chamber through a round hole instead of through a long narrow slit. It seems a small thing; nevertheless, failing to humor nature in so small a thing as that, she would not give him her confidence, and he failed to prove what he was convinced was the truth. He died without the knowledge. But another remedies the defect, and analyzes the sun's ray, and by his successful experiment makes knowledge of what was only theory before.

Well, now, so does faith operate in religion. I believe that God is. My father taught me to believe that. When I saw him upon his knees, and with bare brow, his face turned toward the skies, I felt that in that spectacle I had a sufficient proof for me that there is a God. I must believe it. I could do no other. But with later years I came to God by way of experiment. I began to test by experiment, like Newton, what I had before believed. When a man thus tries God by faith, feeling his way toward the Almighty, he is made over in the image of God, he feels in his heart the movements of the divine life, and takes upon himself all that is communicable of the divine nature. Then by experience he has personal, positive knowledge of what he only believed before.

Now, this capacity is given to man alone, so far as we have a knowledge of the creatures of the universe.

II. Without seeking farther for religious talents, we insist upon these. Here they are, a distinct part of human nature. Their existence must be admitted, except by two classes of persons. There are, first, those upon whom the extreme penalty of the law stated in this text has been executed. Of course such persons cannot discover these talents in themselves, and they are naturally enough disposed to deny that they exist. Such persons will say that they exist only in imagination, that a man can imagine anything he chooses about himself, and that if those who talk of such things were properly educated, they would at once see that there are no distinctly religious faculties in man.

Then there are others who have not gone so far in the experience of loss. These faculties are not yet annihilated by neglect, but they are only dormant. The person may be described as spiritually asleep. As a sleeping man does not know that he has hands or feet, so these persons do not discover in themselves any such talents as I have described. This last is the condition of crowding multitudes of men, both in and out of the church.

Now, how much confidence is to be placed in the judgment of these naturally disqualified persons on this matter? I know some persons who are utterly incapable of carrying on any reasoning process. Other faculties are good in them, but they have no faculty of argument. They cannot take a fact and from it reach a conclusion. They cannot see the force of two facts placed together. Now, suppose such a person should presume to say to some mathematician that man has no reasoning faculties, he knows that he has not, because he cannot understand such a thing as reasoning, and he knows there cannot be any such faculty in himself. What confidence would the mathematician have in his judgment on the matter? He would merely laugh at the simple man. Well, now, is it any more reasonable for men who have neglected the religious nature until, according to the law here stated to us, their faculties for religion have died of neglect, to assert that man has no religious nature, and to fortify the decision by a reference to their own highly cultivated intellect? To all who have not abused their nature, either by scorning all religion, or by going to church for the sake of fashion, where they are never made to search their own hearts, these religious faculties are as genuine and as real as the power to remember or reason is to the philosopher.

III. We come now to the full force of the law stated in the text. We shall only dwell upon the last part of it—the declaration that the neglect to use shall be punished with obliteration.

1. Observe that this is in harmony with Scripture. This text is clear and strong enough. " From him that hath not shall be taken away even that which he hath." This means that from him who uses not. This is in harmony with the figurative style of Scripture. It is in harmony with fact also, for in the true sense a man has only what he uses. " Take therefore the talent from him." That is the saddest word in the universe. It is the declaration of judicial loss by neglect. Again, take the words, " The heart of this people is waxed gross and their ears are dull of hearing, and their eyes they have closed lest at any time they should see with their eyes, and hear with their ears, and should understand with their heart, and should be converted, and I should heal them." This passage appears first in

Isaiah. There it has a form very common in the Old Testament. The person speaking is represented as causing the effects which he describes. In the New Testament the man is represented as himself causing the effects. Now, put the two forms together, and we get the true, full meaning. It comes as a natural result from the man's own neglect, but all the same it is a judicial punishment for the man's neglect of his opportunities and endowments.

2. This result is in harmony with a law which prevails everywhere in the universe. Your property becomes of less value if it is not kept in use. This is the case with every organ of the body. An unused limb soon grows helpless. When a limb is broken, it must remain for some time surrounded with bandages, and the result is that the joints become stiff, and can recover their natural elasticity only by an experience of severe, and often long-continued, pain. Shut all light from the eye and it would soon lose the power to see. I have read of fish in the great mammoth cave of Kentucky, which have no eyes. They are of the same species as other fish in neighboring waters outside the cave, in which the eyes are natural in form and function; but through long generations being shut up in utter darkness, where eyes would be of no use, nature has refused to continue making eyes for them, and only scars are seen where eyes should be. It is the same with the intellect. A faculty unused becomes weak and incompetent for action. When one has had no

opportunities of education in youth, it is with difficulty that he can acquire even the simplest elements of education in after years. I have seen a man of twenty-five making more effort to learn to read words of one syllable than the most of us would require to master a difficult work in science or mathematics. In some states, for many years criminals were shut up in solitary confinement. Thus shut out from all communication with their fellow-beings many of them became idiotic. The intellect, deprived of any proper field of action, was destroyed.

Now, we find that this law prevails in every other sphere into which we may look. Is it not reasonable to suppose that it would also prevail in regard to the faculties upon which religion depends for its existence ? And so much the more as these faculties can find no exercise except in religion ? A man cannot be placed in circumstances in which he will not give some little exercise to the intellect, but his religious nature is never used at all except as he with design devotes himself to God.

3. Experience confirms all that has been said on this subject. Ask a not thoroughly bad man of forty. He tells you that he has no interest in religion. Yet he will speak with a good deal of feeling of the tenderness which he felt when he was a boy and later ; and there will be some pathos in his word and voice as he declares that he wishes that he could have the same feelings now. This tenderness proves that his faculties are not yet destroyed. They are

only dormant. The man is spiritually asleep. If he would bend his attention to the subject, if he would look into his own heart, if he would begin to pray, with the first approach to the throne of God he would find his religious power returning to him again. But let him go on as he has been doing, and when he is seventy years old, ask him again the same searching questions, and he will yet tell you that he feels no interest in these things ; but there will be this difference, the pathos will be gone, there will be no tenderness or regret as he makes the confession that he does not care for these things. He is old, he cannot be far from death, and he knows it ; yet at a time when you would expect him to be most concerned on his prospects for the future, he is indifferent, and shows no signs of feeling. Now, what does this mean but that he has suffered a judicial loss of all power to be religious. He could not become a Christian now. Of course this is an illustrative case, the like to which may be found in actual life. Still many have been saved after seventy who had always neglected religion before. Probably no one's power to be religious is wholly lost, however much it may be impaired, until just before he dies. The Spirit will then cease to strive with man.

Now, if these considerations have any force with your minds, the next thought is what are you going to do about it ? Some of you have been so full of business that you have never found any time for religion.. You are not more tender and susceptible

than you were ten years ago. Will you allow the
process of destruction to go on until there is no
power left in you? That is to be lost. There are many
belonging to one church or another, who use their
church for worldly ends. They would have nothing
to do with it only that it is fashionable to have
a church. They are neglecting their souls under
the most deceptive and dangerous circumstances.
They lose religion in dependence upon a fashionable
church. There can be but one end to this process.

Let us not forget that this loss of power is hell.
It is the true idea of perdition. That means a wast-
ing away. It is simply decay. The only suggestion that can grow out of this study, except that
the punishment of the lost will be eternal, is that
the lost will continue to decay into final and complete extinction. But against this is the fact that
many of the other powers of manhood have grown
strong while the religious nature has been destroyed,
and these other powers have become proportionately
stronger because the higher nature has been allowed
to perish by decay. The intellect will have its full
power and life. It will be vigorous enough to preserve to a man a knowledge of his identity. The
faculties most conspicuous in devils irretrievably
lost are the mental powers. They are not represented as having anything that suggests a religious
faculty. There can be hell enough to a man who
has lost all his religious faculty. No; there is no
where any comfort or encouragement to any who
are neglecting their religious nature.

THE CHOICE OF MOSES ; OR, THE BEST OF SIN vs. THE WORST OF RELIGION.

"By faith Moses, when he was come to years, refused to be called the son of Pharaoh's daughter ; choosing rather to suffer affliction with the people of God, than to enjoy the pleasures of sin for a season." HEBREWS xi. 24, 25.

MOSES again ! Yes, there is so much of Moses that he is not easily exhausted ! Some mountains tower in majestic grandeur, not only above all the plain, but above all other mountains ; so, a few men, in self-contained, God-anointed greatness and power, rise above all other leaders, rulers, and conquerors ! Moses was one of the first, as he yet remains one of the most conspicuous of these remarkable figures.

Just now you are to think of him standing high enough to be seen by all the human race. A great beam is balanced over his head, after the manner of a beam in a pair of scales. To one end is attached all religion, with the very worst that any man can ever experience with it ; to the other is suspended all that in the best circumstances can be realized in a life of sin. Over the head of Moses the balance is being adjusted between these two unfairly

weighted scales. I say unfairly weighted—it is
certainly an exceptional arrangement to weigh all
that is poorest of one thing against all that is best
in another. Generally it is the best against the
best, and the worst against the worst. It cannot be
a fair test that puts the worst of one thing against
the best of another. Yet so balanced, over the head
of Moses, influenced by his whole thought and life,
the beam inclines decidedly on the side of religion.
Its worst is better than the best that a life of sin
can give.

Now, we are indebted to Moses for this discovery.
He was so situated that he might have had in per-
petuity all the best side of a life of sin. He might
have enjoyed "the pleasures of sin for a season."
It was also true that as the times then were, and as
he was situated, if he chose God and His people, he
could only realize the worst that can come from a
religious life. Yet he turned his back upon these
"pleasures of sin," and chose to "suffer affliction
with the people of God." This remarkable choice
has balanced these two over against each other to
so stand forever in the eye of the world in an
eternal affirmation that the very best that any man
can realize from a life of sin is less to be desired
than the very worst that can ever be experienced
from a life of devotion to God and fellowship with
his people.

I say we are indebted to Moses for this convincing
testimony. Nowhere else are the strong claims of

12

religion set forth so irresistibly. This act of his was a typical act for the benefit of all the ages. It appeals to us here now. There is not one of us who may not consider this matter with advantage to himself. What multitudes think of religion, feel that they need it, intend well, but put off any personal devotion to it from year to year, their life meanwhile speeding on! Religious desire fades away into indifference. Indifference hardens often into actual opposition. The capacity to receive any impression from the Holy Spirit is wholly lost. Then pretty soon, in an unexpected hour, death comes along and knocks the man off the pedestal on which he has boasted that he could stand forever, and his soul is damned.

To avert so great a calamity, let me urge you to choose religion as the basis of your life structure.

I. I will first turn your thought to the very worst aspect in which religion can be placed before you in asking your acceptance.

1. The worst that can be said of it is that it may cause you to experience affliction. That includes all worldly loss and persecution, and injury to character and person, and martyrdom.

Certainly some men have found that the beginning of a religious life was to them the beginning of a life of trials. So many have suffered on account of their professing the Christian faith that the Church seems to the eye of the world as the chosen mark at which all the arrows of evil design

have been aimed in times past. It seems, in many
periods of its history, to have drunk to the dregs a
bitter cup more than full. So many have suffered
the spoiling of their goods, and the loss of their lives,
on account of their profession, that the Christian
Church seems distinguished in history by its afflictions.

Then, in addition to these facts, there are some
passages of Scripture which seem to indicate that
it is the will of God, that those who profess faith in
Him shall suffer persecution. Such are the words
of the psalmist: " Many are the afflictions of the
righteous "; and the words of Jesus, " In the world
ye shall have tribulation "; and those of Paul, " If
ye be without chastisement, then are ye bastards
and not sons."

Now, putting these facts and these words together,
it is stating the matter with sufficient mildness to
say that if you embrace the religion of Christ you
may find some affliction in consequence of your
profession.

2. But it is necessary to the truth to say also
that you may not have affliction on account of your
faith and profession.

It is certainly wrong to regard suffering as an
inevitable consequence of an attachment to Christ.
Many have the idea that it is a sad thing for any
one to become a Christian. They associate a religious life with the loss of everything that makes
life in this world desirable. It seems to them that

to espouse the cause of Christ will be to lie down
upon a bed of sorrows, and to awaken again to
sorrow and pain. They will dwell in a land of
shadows, and hold fellowship with all that is dark
and melancholy. But this is a very much exag-
gerated view of the possibilities in the way of affliction that lie in the path of the Christian profession.
Why, that was not true of Christ's people in the
darkest ages of the Church's history. Even when
the Church was passing through the hottest fires all
did not burn. All were not martyrs. All did not suffer
loss. It is true that all would suffer more or less in
such times from the fearful apprehension of what
might fall upon them. Every day they would drag
the heavy hours along, pressed under the burden-
some thought that they knew not in what hour
they might be dragged to their death. This was
certainly bad enough. But these fears would be
greatly relieved by that hope which burns eternal in
the human breast, that they might wholly escape.
Every day that passed without harm would only
make the hope take a stronger hold upon them.
But even when persecuting fires were hottest, farther
than this fear of what might come, the greater
number of the Christians suffered no more than if
they had never heard of Christ. We overlook this
fact in reading the history of the Church in the
past. It is very much like this. We read that the
cholera is spreading with tremendously fatal results
in Spain. Thousands have already died, and thou-

sands more are sure to go. When Spain is mentioned, therefore, we at once think of cholera, and
associate the idea of fearful danger with the name
of this land, though as a matter of fact the danger
has not been near the vast mass of the Spanish
people. Where one has died ten thousand and more
have not been in any danger. But all the same,
everyone is all the time distressed with the fear
that it may come near to them. Now, that is just
the way it is with the Church. We remember the
cases where great tribulations have been endured
because of a profession of the faith of Christ, but
we are unmindful of the much greater number of
those who have not suffered at all.

In the same way we are to understand the passages of Scripture which paint so dark a lot in this
world for those who make a profession of Christ's
name. They relate not to each individual, but to
the Church as a whole. Those spoken of by Christ
and the disciples referred to a time that was then
near at hand when the people of God should pass
through some dark days. They meant no more
than that during these days so many should suffer for
Christ's name that it would seem as if anyone could
not bear His name without falling under the rod of
affliction. But these words did not mean that
everyone who should take upon him the name of
Christ should be persecuted. To make them bear
this meaning would expose them to contradiction by
facts that are known to all. All the early believers

do not rest in martyr's graves, down in the deep
silence of the catacombs.   No, the Scriptures do not
teach that all individual believers will fall under
persecution, or special affliction, on account of their
faith.   It is true of by far the greatest number of
those who have borne the Christian name that they
have had no greater trials in this world than if they
had not borne the name of Christ at all.   It is true
of those who are Christians to-day.   The novice may
feel the sting of his companion's ridicule and the
sneer of godless men.   Temptations to commit sin,
which he would not have felt as a trial before, because he would not have resisted them, will torment
him now ; but farther than this he feels no reproach in the cross to-day.   Christian men grow
rich, and suffer poverty, side by side with those who
make no acknowledgment of Christ and His cause.
They enjoy vigorous health in person or family, or
die indiscriminately in the same atmosphere.   So
that there is nothing in the facts to justify us in believing that as anyone commits himself to God and
His cause, he is set upon as marked for special dis-
pensations of affliction.

So while we warn you that a profession of faith
in Christ may lead to your suffering some afflictions,
it is just as true that you may never have any such
experience.   God holds in His hands the power, and
reserves to Himself the right to afflict any of
His people for the discipline of their character, or as
an example to others of patience in trials, or as an

exhibition of the power of His grace to sustain under great tribulations. Hence each believer should be warned that this may fall to his lot; but he should also know that this is the worst that ever comes with a life of faith in the Redeemer.

Now, here is the worst side. If you turn to Christ you may have afflictions, or you may not.

II. We turn now to the other side, that is to the best a man can have if he determines to live in sin.

1. There is first the fact that he may have a life of pleasure—"The pleasures of sin for a season "—this is what is offered.

1. There may be pleasure in a life of sin. Sometimes it is said by some earnest advocate of religion, that there is no pleasure in sin—this is a mistake in every way. It is no recommendation to religion to tell a person that he finds no pleasure in the manner of life which he lives, when his own senses contradict what you say. That advocacy will not advance religion. A man may say that he himself finds no pleasure in a certain course, but he has no right to say that no other finds pleasure in it. A godly man may well say that he finds no pleasure in sin, just as a vile man may say that he finds no pleasure in a prayer-meeting. The fact is that there is pleasure in both to the person whose tastes qualify him to enter into it. You may find a company of men and women reading and talking about the Word of God. They also bow down in prayer. They lift radiant faces. They do not seem to want enjoyment in

their employment. Yet many persons will look
upon them with pity because they have no more
exciting mode of pleasure than that. Again you
may find a company spending the flying hours amid
the gaieties of a fashionable ball-room. They dance,
they drink, they jest and trifle, and they certainly
find pleasure in that mode of spending their time.
Another would not perhaps find any pleasure there ;
but they do, and it is absurd to say that there is no
pleasure in such pursuits. Take a man who is fast
running down the scale through drunkenness.
There is nothing but ruin before him. He sees the
disgrace of his family, the degradation of himself
until his own children shall with difficulty not despise him. His own life is also at stake. No one
knows all this better than he. Yet he drinks, and
goes down on his knees to beg for drink. He will
lie in a manner that would once have shocked him
as being the gate of hell. All this he will do, and
then are you going to tell him that there is no
pleasure in his sin ? It may be that now it has become a dreary pleasure ; but it is the feeding of the
inextinguishable and insatiable fires of an appetite
that seems to have written itself upon every fibre
of his muscular and nervous being. Even yet all
the pleasure he is capable of receiving is found in
the drink. But he remembers a time when the
drink meant all delights. The rousing company,
the high excitement, the mirth, the brilliancy, everything that a man could desire was found in the
drink and associated with it.

No, there is no use of telling anyone that there is no pleasure in sin.

There are two classes who may deny that there is any pleasure in sin. There are some who say this dogmatically, because they are unwilling to allow anything to those who are on a different side from themselves. Such persons try, some of them, to sweep everything before them by mere force of will. Their advocacy will not help any cause, except among those who are incapable of thinking, or of forming any opinion from facts which all may observe.

But still some others may say the same thing because they speak comparatively. They speak truly their own experience. They know what sin is. They have drained its cup. Then when they had proven all its sweets, they turned to Christ. They have walked in the path of the Christian long enough to know what it can give. They have not forgotten what their old life was. In comparing the past with the present they find their walk with Christ so much more pure, and dignified, and sure as to the results, that they say that in comparison with what they now enjoy there is no pleasure in sin, and in speaking thus they are certainly true.

2. But now having fairly admitted that there is pleasure in sin, you must guard against believing more than the truth on this subject. It is not admitted that there is pleasure in every form of sin. The text does not say anything of that kind. It

only admits that a person may find a life of pleasure in a life of sin. But then he may not. There is just as much uncertainty about this as there is about finding affliction with Christ and His people. On one side it must be said that you may find affliction with the people of God, and you may find pleasure in a life of sin. But there is some uncertainty on both of these things. Then on the other hand you may go with God and His people and escape any special affliction altogether, and you may live a life of sin and not find it a life of pleasure.

3. Then notice what it is you get with sin. It is only pleasure in the best case. You do not get peace. Now, the difference between peace and pleasure is so great that it should not go unnoticed. Pleasure is only a ripple on the surface of the waters, peace is that profound calm that reaches to the very depths. Pleasure is the surface joy that makes lambs leap in the field, and kittens purr by the fire; but peace is the persuasion of innocence, or of safety, that makes a man calm and self-possessed, when death, under arms, stands at his door. It is the man appointed to martyrdom asleep. It is the child's innocence.

4. Then notice that it is only the pleasures of sin " for a season." They are not a permanent possession. They will not last a man his lifetime, but only while the body maintains its vigor; and they, more than work or study, will hasten to undermine that vigor. When the man begins to break down, the

pleasure is at an end. Oh, I think of boys and young men, smoking and drinking, and when they say that it makes them feel better, every man of experience knows that that is true, but it is drawing upon capital all the time. A young man has $50,000 at five per cent. There are $2,500 for him to live upon every year. But he forms extravagant habits and tastes. He can spend $5,000 per annum. I expostulate with him. But he says, "I feel better than if I spent only $2,500." Now, I do not doubt that; but I am thinking about his future when his capital will be all gone. At the end of four years he will have less than $40,000 capital. In a little more than fifteen years his fortune will be all wasted. Yet that is just what so many are doing with the strength of their bodies.

III. Now, let us set this matter fairly before the mind. Take religion at the worst. You stand in the glorious company of Paul, and Peter, and Polycarp, and Perpetua, and Wickliffe, and Calvin, and Wesley, and Lady Huntington, and Bishop Simpson, and Spurgeon, and Queen Victoria, and indeed of all the people you most honor, both living and dead. Take those whom you wish to be like in old age, and when you come to die; every one of them is found in this class. Did not religion make these persons great and noble as they are in your esteem? Would Queen Victoria be what she is in the admiration of the world without the profession of Christ? Indeed, instead of that she

might be no more loved than a Brunehaut or a
Fredegonde.   It is something to me that I am
building my character and life upon the same plan
as that which has made the greatest and best people
what they were.

But turn to the other side and what do you see?
A widely different class.   Here you join the company of Vitellius, and Cleopatra, and Nero, and Lollia
Paulina, and Charles II., and Aaron Burr, and the
people of the style of Madame DuBarry, and all
those whom you intend and desire least of anything
to be like.   You shrink from any resemblance to
them in age ; for the world, you would not lie on
their bed in death.

Would not religion have saved these from being
such people that contempt grows rank at the mention of their names ?   What they were in a great
place, any of us will be in our little sphere, if we
build upon the same principles.

I said in beginning this sermon that the scales
were unfairly weighted.   Instead of putting the
worst of religion against the best of a life of sin, let
us put the average of the one against the average
of the other.   Then, if the balance turns decidedly
in favor of religion, when this is weighed at a dis-
advantage, what must be the determination when
the two are weighed on equal and fair terms ?   In
that case I ask you to choose religion probably without any violence of persecution, with the growing
respect and confidence of mankind, with a con-

stantly extending influence in the world, with an
envied position in society, with purity and peace
in your own heart, and happiness and security in
your home, ripening into age with a crown upon
your brow, and a sceptre of ever-increasing power
in your hand. This is not an extravagant represen-
tation of what you may find in a religious life, but
is a quite common experience in the Church of
to-day. It is exemplified in the lives of the majority
of Christians whom you see around you.

It is only fair also to put the opposite side of the
question in different colors. Instead of pleasure in
sin, suppose I say a life of sin without any distin-
guishing pleasures, but instead consumed by envy
and jealousy, filled with a growing spirit of fretful-
ness, discontent, and complaint against everybody
and everything. Finally the health is broken down
by excesses, and the nerves, shattered, are screaming
out in constant pain, and the whole body, as the
years pass, is increasing the food for corruption.
The mind has long been like a cage of unclean birds,
and is a prey to foul and vicious thoughts. The
soul's special gifts have all disappeared as the judicial punishment of neglect, until it has no power to
will a good thing, or to desire a pure thing. Thus
festering and tormented under the weight of his
own sins, the poor man, a pest to himself, drags
along his weary way to the grave, illustrating in
himself the words used to describe the condition of
the world at a former time :

" On that hard pagan world, disgust
   And secret loathing fell,
Deep weariness and sated lust
   Made human life a hell.

" In his cool hall, with haggard eyes
   The Roman noble lay ;
He drove abroad in furious guise
   Along the Appian way ;

" He made a feast, drank fierce and fast,
   And crowned his hair with flowers,
No easier and no quicker passed
   The impracticable hours."

Now, this is not an imaginary picture of what a man may experience in a life of sin. It may be seen around you every day. It is true of many whom you know well. They have ridden the life of sin, and it has done well for them for a time, but at last their capacity to receive pleasure from it has been worn out; and then, like Absalom's mule, it has walked off from under them, when it has discovered that they were caught by the hair.

IV. Now, I urge upon you the importance of a conscious choice between these two at once. It is a man's duty to decide the grave affairs of life for himself, and not leave them to settle themselves. This will settle itself if you do not settle it by a conscious choice, and if it settles itself you will find yourself in the end on the side of sin, without ever having intended it. It is just as it is with a boy, in choosing a calling in life. He may decide to pursue some line of work for a lifetime, and then may apply himself to it, working himself up to its requirements, and gradually rising to competency, respectability and influence, while another says about such an important matter, " I will wait, I am young, there is no hurry," and so leaving the matter it settles itself, and he just drifts along through life, taking hold upon anything which comes to hand, and is like a piece of driftwood in a stream.   Yet that is just the last thing which he thought to be like. He says, when fifty years of age, and he sees his former schoolmate in a high and influential position, " Put me in his place and I could do as well as he." But he cannot be put there.   It is impossible.   The time is gone by.   Each of these men put himself where he finds himself at fifty.   At twenty years of age the one chose an honorable calling, and the other said, " I will not be in a hurry."   He waited, and it settled itself as such things always do, and in a manner that now furnishes him a great surprise.

Now, this is just the case with those who do not choose . Christ and a religious life.   The matter settles itself, and they will be greatly surprised in the hour of death, and in the day of judgment.   Then as dark horrors come out to meet them, they will cry out in alarm and despair.   This is not what they intended their life to end in.

1. Now, a person *can* choose.   But you say, " It is almost impossible.   I feel no interest."   It is a difficult thing to do indeed.   It is difficult because one must call his religious faculties into exercise in making this choice, and these faculties have been so much

neglected that they do not act easily. After you have done no work for some time it is very hard to get your body into working order. So with these faculties. This act of choosing Christ is the first distinct act that a man does with these faculties. It is not surprising that he finds it difficult to act. It would be surprising if he found it easy. It is like the man with the withered hand. The hardest thing that that man ever did was to try to raise up that hand. After he had once tried he found that he could do almost anything with that hand. It did not cost him as much effort to use that hand all the rest of his life as it did to raise it up that one time. This act of choice is the letting of one's religious faculties out of prison. It is lifting a great weight off from a spring, so that it may rebound naturally. The letting one out of prison is not doing all his work, but it is putting him in a position to do his work. So is making the choice to be a Christian. After that prayer and every other duty will become easy.

2. I urge this choice upon you because it is necessary to realize your true destiny. Had Moses not made the choice he did, the world would have ceased to remember him ages ago. God would have delivered His people by another hand. But did not God raise up Moses for this particular work? Yes, most certainly. Can a man raised up for a particular work, fail to accomplish it? Yes, certainly. Why, look at the work done by many great men. Take one example—that of Bonaparte. In any case he must have been a leader among men, but do you

suppose that God raised him up to do the work of desolation which he did? You cannot believe that. Just what things he was designed in the plans of God to do we cannot tell, but when we see Europe given over to absolutism for more than half a century through his acts, we cannot avoid the conviction that he was a man who missed his destiny. Through his hand, Italy, which for centuries had been taking lessons in self-government, was prostrated under the heels of tyrants, and its people struggled against their adverse fate for between sixty and seventy years before they could undo the wrong that was done to them chiefly by Bonaparte. Now it was in his power to have advanced civilization a century; instead of that he put it back for a century. There must have been some mistaken choice in his life to work out such disastrous results. So might Moses have made a mistaken choice, and have fallen short of his true work and destiny. So may you. You cannot tell what great things God may have in His plan for your life. Do not defeat those plans by a mistaken choice now.

3. But you cannot know! You are all in the dark as to your future! So was Moses when he made this choice. So is every man when he makes the chief decision of his life. I do not say that God designs you to be a great reformer of abuses, but I do say that you ought to put yourself right so that God can use you in his own way, whether it be in a little or great sphere. The choice must be made in faith, and in trust for the future.

13

PRESENT KNOWLEDGE DEFECTIVE.

"For we know in part, and we prophesy in part : but when that which is perfect is come, then that which is in part shall be done away."--1 CORINTHIANS xiii. 9, 10.

LET us notice the fact stated that our knowledge is defective.

II. Let us seek after a satisfactory reason for this fact.

III. Let us apply this reason to some departments of knowledge in which we particularly desire fuller knowledge.

I. No statement is more safe than that human knowledge is at best very imperfect. It commands but a narrow view, and cannot see far in advance. There are two fields in which human knowledge experiences constant humiliation.

1. First, there is the great domain of nature. Men know just enough of the material universe to understand that they have scarcely penetrated beneath the surface. It is true that the men of to-day are far in advance of those who lived in former times. They were poor indeed. One thousand years ago, the most enlightened men might have said, " We know in part," in comparison with well-taught children who live to-day. But all the pride

of science is abased when once we think of the unturned pages in nature's great book, of which men have as yet deciphered but the title page and some small portion of its table of contents.

2. Then there is the Book of Divine Revelation. There human knowledge is humbled still more. Into many boundless realms it opens the door just a little way, far enough indeed to fill us with adoring wonder, and to captivate us with the desire of knowing all, but not widely enough to enable us to enter and explore all. In what great darkness we are left on many subjects of the weightiest import when we have read it all! For example, we feel that it has not told us half of what we desire to know concerning God. As to His nature and man's, and especially concerning our future, there come surging against us like the great waves of the sea,

> "The same old baffling questions. O my friend,
> I cannot answer them, in vain I send
> My soul into the dark, where never burn
> The lamps of science, nor the natural light
> Of reason's sun and stars. I cannot learn
> Their great and solemn meanings, nor discern
> The awful secrets of the eyes that turn
> Ever more on us through the day and night.
>
>   *   *   *
>
> I have no answer for myself and thee,
> Save that I learned beside my mother's knee :
> All is of God that is, and is to be,
> And God is good. Let this suffice us, still
> Resting in childlike trust upon His will
> Who moves to His great ends unthwarted by the ill."

II. Now, can we find any reasonable explanation of these limitations to our knowledge? Why is the little we do know shut in on every side by darkening walls? Since God has given a revelation to the world, why is not its knowledge more full? After He has opened the doors, why should we yet have to say, "We know only in part?" In the past a common answer to this question has been that our ignorance is necessary to uncrown the soaring pride of man's heart by letting him feel that he cannot compass all things. It has also been often said that it is a deserved reproof to prying curiosity. An example of this species of answer is found in the narrative of a Sunday School teacher's perplexity. A boy in her class had been reading in the New Testament of people walking on the roofs of houses. Now, he had never seen anything but the pitched roofs so common in our latitudes, and there the record seemed to indicate what could not be possible in fact. He was face to face with a great difficulty in interpretation. According to his age and development, the difficulty was as great, the obstacle as insuperable as those by which some men have been cast hopeless wrecks upon the rocks of infidelity. However, he went to his teacher for an explanation of the apparent contradiction between narrative and fact. She did what she could. She simply put him off by saying that he must receive the Scriptures on faith, and not indulge any unholy questionings as to their deep meanings and difficult points. Now, the superin-

tendent heard the answer, and afterwards said to
the teacher, " You did not give the right answer to
that question ? " " No ! " she said, " What ought I
to have answered ? " " Why," said he, " The things
that are impossible to men are possible to God."

Now, that style of answer is not sufficient, because
from first to last it is entirely wrong. Why, it seems
to me that I would not be puffed up with vain pride,
but would be truly humbled if in my thought I
could walk right up to the Deity's blazing throne
and look upon His infinite nature, and if my eye
could sweep out intelligently over His boundless
universe, understanding the circumstances and conditions of life, and in some measure sympathizing
with the sins and conflicts, and sorrows and
triumphs of other rational creatures even apart
from my own race! And I am sure that I would
not experience the inflation that springs merely
from the gratification of an unholy curiosity ; but
rather that a feeling of fervent gratitude would fill
my heart if I could know now all that my little
being shall be, when at some time in the future it
shall be perfected and glorified through Christ's redeeming work. I know that my tears of thankful
exultation and rapturous praise would fall upon the
dear cross as never before.

And if there were no better reason for withholding
knowledge than simply to humiliate us, I believe
from what we know of God in other things, it would
be like Him to give us the fullest knowledge we
could desire.

We must seek elsewhere the reason of our necessary ignorance. Undoubtedly the prophet's explanation is found in man's incapacity. We reach this
conclusion from all possible analogies in the case.
All knowledge is gained by man subject to two
hindrances.

1. In the natural world knowledge is limited by
man's ability to ascend originally through the various
progressive steps by which the result is reached.
For example, during all ages, ever since Adam's day,
men have been affected by what we call the law of
gravitation ; but it was not until Newton's day
that the growing intelligence of the race had reached
a culminating point, from which one man stretched
high enough up to generalize from many facts the
one underlying principle. Since then men have
recognized this law.

We know enough indeed, to know continually that
there are truths and facts beating against us and
breaking upon us all the time, and yet they leave us
as little informed as waves that break on unknown
shores. Prof. Tyndall has lately shown that in light
are some beams which are black to our eyes. Now,
scarcely anything could be more contradictory to
our common ideas than that the light can have some
beams that are black, though it is commonly known
that any painter will add a dash of lamp-black to
his white lead in order to produce a more perfect
white. Well, these black beams had been constantly
beating upon men through all the ages ; they had

been acting upon the philosophers who were busy investigating the truths of nature; they had poured through the eye of Newton, who made light a special subject of study, and who advanced farther into the knowledge of its character than any others had ever done; but they remained undiscovered. No man had yet risen high enough into the ethereal blue of infinite intelligence to follow up the various steps in experimental investigations and uncover the hiding-place of these rays until Dr. Tyndall drew aside their covering. And so it is with all discovery. After ages of ignorant groping, someone gathers in himself the intelligent fruition of all past time, and takes the original steps that uncover some deep hidden mystery, and "The energy sublime of a century bursts full-blossomed on the thorny stem of time." Of how many things we are ignorant which will be familiarly known to those who live after us, when someone has taken the original steps necessary to pour the revelations of the truth upon men's minds!

2. The second hindrance to the attainment of knowledge is the inability to understand it after it has been once fully discovered. This is the cause of one's not learning more from divine revelation. We have not the capacity to understand all that God has written for our instruction. In this we are as children at every stage of their mental progress. A small child may be able to remember the forms and names of the letters of the alphabet; but it requires

a higher intelligence to analyze the several sounds of those letters, and then to combine them into words and sentences. One who can do this last can read, yet he is not capable of being interested in heavy philosophical writings, or of reading intelligently the best poetry the ages have produced. A boy may have an intelligence high enough to learn and repeat the multiplication table, and yet be quite incompetent to understand a demonstration in Euclid which is quite simple to many others. Now, suppose some of these children should say, "If men write mathematics and philosophy and poetry at all, why do they not use such words as will make them simple, or make their explanations full enough for us to comprehend them? Why are not trigonometry, and the calculus, and Plato, and Leibnitz, and Shakespeare and Tennyson so simply written that we can read them with interest?" It is very plain that in these cases the answer would be, that though the child can understand some things, there are others which are beyond him, and though written as simply as language can make them, still everyone will not have the capacity to read and understand them.

Now, the same is true of much that God has spoken in revelation. A great truth pours all its light upon men: but they do not apprehend it because they have not the natural capacity to take it in, or they have never yet been brought into the particular circumstances under which, in the nature of the case, it would be fully understood. Because of this fact, it is true that the Bible has been as much a progressive revelation to mankind as have the discoveries in nature from one age to another. Indeed, the Bible as a revelation is progressive as to the individual. Its doors swing more widely open just as a man's capacity grows, or as his spiritual understanding rises to a higher plane. Some deep affliction, or great sorrow, leads you to see the enlarged meaning of a promise which never before had arrested your attention, or had taken hold upon your heart. In age, or want, you see the grand scope of passages to which in youth you gave a very narrow interpretation.

And this revelation is also progressive with the ages. New pages in the book are turned by time. The prophets had fuller light than the patriarch; and, except as they were exalted by direct inspiration, we can go deeper and see a wider view than the prophets. Abraham might have said "I know only in part" in comparison with many children who live now; and the most enlightened high priest in the sacred temple never understood the grand and far-reaching significance of his highly typical system of religion as does an intelligent Sunday School teacher of the present day.

III. Let us now apply this explanation of man's ignorance to some departments of knowledge where we particularly desire to know more.

1. How does this idea of our incapacity explain

our ignorance of God? On no subject do we more
desire an enlargement of our knowledge. We have
certain forms of words, such as, "the Trinity in
Unity," and "three Persons and one God." They
do not convey a very clear impression to our minds,
nor do we very well know just what we mean when
we use them. We feel that any attempt to get
under them is like trying to leap over a rock and
striking against the face of it, and falling back
bruised and broken; and so when we have read or
repeated these expressions we leave them with the
councils and the schoolmen, and our hungry hearts
send many a questioning word throbbing against
the distant echoing sky, asking that we may know
more of His manner of existence—how He can
know all things, and be ever-present everywhere—
how He can care for all the crowding multitudes of
His countless hungry children.

But we are told that we are not great enough to
comprehend these things from any revelation of
them that could possibly be made. To understand
this is only to understand that God's great life is
inconceivably greater than our life. We can only
understand another existence by what we know of
our own. God's existence is so much beyond our
own that we cannot rise to comprehend it. We see
something like this in a child's effort to understand
the life of a man. Your babe upon its mother's
knee, your growing boy, does not know the mystery
and inspiration of the great life a man or woman

lives, because his own life is not large enough to enable him to enter into it. I remember when friends and relatives used patronizingly to lay their hands upon our heads and say, " Enjoy yourselves— make the most of the present, for you are seeing your best days now ; " but it is a very small conception of life which regards childhood as the best of it. Why, as for myself, I know that I experience a clinging to life, and a delight in its labors and objects and aims, beyond all expression more strong and intense than anything I ever knew in the bright but empty days of childhood. A child's life finds its fulness of joy in the simple pleasures of a passing holiday. How can such a life measure the life of a man or woman that reaches around the world, leaps into the distant future, and stretches away to the far-off skies above him ? I remember when we were boys we spent many a glad holiday in the street, and we would dig a small cave, about as large as our hats, under the ledge of a bank, and then we would make a hole through the sod from the top down into the cave, and put a stick through the hole, and pile small lumps of earth around the stick, and then we would sit there and shove the stick up and down, and the lumps would be ground into fine dust, and our faces would be covered with it, and our clothes penetrated and filled with it. We called these our mills, and said we were millers, and felt very proud to be all covered with the dust like whitened millers ; but who cannot see that such

millers as we were, were quite incapable of understanding from such mills the great milling business
represented by the vast elevators in any city where
grain is shipped in large quantities. And as it is in
this, so it is in everything as between the man and
the child, and as the child cannot understand the
man, so much less can we understand God, through
the clearest possible revelation that can ever be
made of Him. Yet as the child approaches to manhood he enters more fully into all the thoughts and
plans of a man, so in like manner, as we become
spiritual, refined and pure, we become better able to
understand God's great nature and life.

It is very much like this. Some of the lower
animals understand some part of man's life. I
know a lady who has taught her parrot to kiss
her. There seems to be a good understanding between them. There is much the same friendly
relation between the Indian and his dog, and the
Arab and his horse. They are intimate companions.
Those dumb brutes obey their masters, and in a
certain sense they love them and cover them with
caressing fondness ; but they do not understand and
know them entirely. Indeed, none of us would feel
flattered if we thought those creatures could fully
comprehend the life of their master and mistress.
We would feel that our life must be cast upon as
low a plane as theirs ; but we know better than that.
We know that the knowledge these animals can have
of us stops just where the best part of us begins.

They understand something of our animal nature. That is nearest to them. It is most like the animal life which alone they live, and as far as their animal life is like ours, there are some points of contact between us, and they rise up into communion with us ; but as soon as we touch the intellectual and rise into the spiritual part of our natures, these creatures are shut out entirely from all sympathy and communion with us.

Now, so it is between us and God. We can understand any revelation of Himself so far as we share His nature, so far as we are like Him. A good man can understand God's goodness. One who is pure readily reads with correctness the revelation of God as so pure that the skies are unholy in his presence. One who loves humanity and delights in messages of helpfulness toward all men can understand that revelation of God which represents Him as loving all the world. Knowing "the love of Christ which passeth knowledge," we shall be "filled with all the fulness of God" (Eph. iii. 19). When, then, we shall rise and be wholly freed from everything that is out of harmony with His nature, we shall know Him and see Him as He is. The revelation will then have greatly progressed, and we will read with wonder great and mighty unfoldings of truth we never saw in it before.

Here, then, is our explanation. We know no more of God than we do, because He is so much greater than we, that our nature—our life—gives us no sufficient key by which to understand Him. Our capacities are not equal to Him.

And I am sure we must be satisfied that it is better so. If in the present condition of our minds we could understand God perfectly, we would cease to reverence Him. We should be led, like Lucifer, to contend with Him for the pre-eminence. We know that this is the effect upon us in all cases that are in any degree analogous. Not long ago some European author said of Gladstone : "He is the greatest statesman of his nation. He is the greatest statesman of his age. He is the greatest statesman of any age." Let it be granted that the words are true, yet the youngest member of the House of Commons can fully understand that greatness, and sitting in his obscure seat, his voice untried in that great arena of intellectual conflict, he may yet realize that it is possible for himself to rise to a pinnacle of equal greatness, and may dream of accomplishing as much.

The fact that he can so understand the greatest statesman of his age prevents his being overmastered by any feeling of reverence for so great a man. So would it be with us toward God if we understood Him fully : but the fact that only as we progress in goodness is His great nature unveiled to us provides for continued reverence, fear and obedience in us, as well as a constant prompting to higher attainments in virtue.

2. There is another field in which we naturally desire a great enlargement of our knowledge—that

is, our future state ; what will it be ? What is the
present condition of our dead ? How little the
Bible teaches us on this subject! And yet we feel
that it could not but be helpful to us to have an
answer to a thousand questions which fear, and
affection, and hope, and sorrow project toward that
unseen world ! And it seems so reasonable that we
should have this help. Why is it denied us ? Here,
as in the other case, we are thrown back upon the
answer that God withholds because we are not
capable of receiving. There is nothing in us by
which we can fully understand what that heavenly
life will be.

To realize this, let us remember how imperfectly
we understand ourselves in the life we now live.
The human intellect, as a subject of study, has
for ages engaged the best thoughts of the greatest
minds, yet the student new to this subject is far
from finding a plain path before him. Then our
senses are but imperfectly understood. Only a
novice will regard them as infallible. " It must be
so, I saw it with my own eyes," is a common expression, as though it must be the end of all doubt,
and the seal of all certainty ; but actually sight,
as well as all the other senses, is often deceived,
and where positively accurate results are sought, as
in scientific research in the laboratory, the senses
are constantly doubted, and their declarations are
submitted to other tests for certification. They who
know the senses best trust them least, so that we

do not perfectly understand this life we are now living so far as our senses are concerned. How much less such a life may to our thought seem possible if we were only more perfect than we are! Then, again, our thoughts are quite limited as to the number of our senses.

We know of five senses, and regard each as an avenue of knowledge; and we vainly think we have sounded all the depths of our being in detecting these five senses. But what if our being is capable of branching out and unfolding until not only five but ten times five senses may discover themselves to us. each with an appropriate sphere of knowledge! All this is possible, and yet how incapable we are of understanding the life we would live on a scale so enlarged! There is an infinity in our natures which our race has but little suspected in the past. I am thinking of some experiments in mind reading which I have witnessed, and which, to all human appearance, were above any suspicion of collusion or deception. These experiments suggest to me that there are in our natures hidden avenues through which thought and feeling may flow, and which none of our studies have yet in any large degree explored. Though we do not comprehend, much less attempt, to explain these phenomena, we are willing to receive from them the suggestion of new possibilities of life in us above anything we have ever begun to experience here, but which we may enter upon and possess as soon as we are emancipated from the enslaving folds of our flesh, with its encompassing weaknesses and imperfections. If, as many things seem to indicate, disembodied spirits know anything about us here, is it not more than probable that they are not shut up to the slow processes of gaining knowledge to which we are accustomed, but that they have access to these hidden avenues of communication in which the flow of thought, feeling and emotion is much more rapid than anything we know of as we now are? And we may not easily reject the thought that evil spirits have over us the great advantage which they do undoubtedly possess through a knowledge of these hidden avenues of our being; and that they would destroy us beyond remedy or hope were we not guarded and preserved by those ministering spirits who, as guardian angels, watch over our destiny, and who equally enjoy all secret knowledge of the great mysteries of our being.

But, you say, much of this is mere speculation. Yes, it is true, but when we cannot know, nothing remains for us but to speculate. It is our only way of getting beyond the narrow limits that confine us. Truly we may say,

" I am, how little more I know!
Whence came I? Whither do I go?
A centred self that feels and is!
A cry between the silences!
A shadow, birth of clouds at strife
With sunshine on the hills of life!

14

A shaft from nature's quiver cast
Into the future from the past !
Between the cradle and the shroud,
A meteor's flash, from cloud to cloud !"

How then is it possible for us to comprehend all
the mystery and meaning of our great life, when
we are entirely freed from the limitations we now
feel in the flesh, when every child shall be greater
than Newton was; when each shall tower into a
lofty realm of intelligence above the most advanced
of living men, and all shall move on together
toward higher revelations and attainments, pressing forward with mighty volume and power, like a
great current sweeping on where single drops could
not move !

We " know in part " then, only because our
capacities are limited. We have no eye to see, nor
ear to hear what heaven is through any revelation
of it that could be possibly made. Our knowledge
will grow as we move toward perfection. Revelation
becomes more complete as the race developes and
progresses towards a more perfect manhood. There
is one word, edification, which in its early Latin
form means to build, and with us means to be informed, to receive an increase of knowledge. So
that our race is being edified, that is, built up. Our
past history and our present position properly is
simply manhood in process of construction, and
when the perfection is reached partial knowledge
shall be done away. A watcher waits through the

weary night, often longing for rest and release. At
last weary eyes look out of an eastern window and
a line of grey stretches all along the sky. Now
she knows that relief is near. The morning is at
hand. An hour later she flings wide the curtain,
turns out her artificial light and is ready to go; but
the grey line that gave her encouragement an hour
ago is all gone. It was swallowed up in the overflowing effulgence of the glad, beautiful morning.
That line was our imperfect knowledge. When
that which is perfect is come it shall be done away;
swallowed up in the overflowing brightness of a full
revelation perfectly understood.

1. With all our imperfect knowledge there are
some things which we do know well. We are as
certain as we can be that we are sinners, and we are
guilty before God. We need pardon and regeneration to be fitted for heaven. And Christ has died
to put this mercy within our reach. Through His
merit we may at once come into a meetness for the
heavenly life. All this we can know without any
further development.

2. These studies should impress upon us the
importance of living in and cultivating our spiritual
natures, since it is by growing in them that fuller
knowledge on many subjects is to be unfolded to us,
and it can be communicated in no other way. So,
to live in prayer, and to come nigh to God in deep,
true faith, is to know God.

3. These studies should help us to patience in our

present worldly circumstances. One of the hard things in life is the inequality in the outward circumstances of those who are equally worthy. The cramping of poverty, the struggles and sufferings of weakness are among the perplexing things. They beat upon us all in some degree.

" Sweet are the scents and sounds of spring,
   And bright are the summer flowers,
   And chill are the autumn winds that bring
   The winter's lingering hours.

" And the world goes round and round,
   And the sun sinks into the sea,
   But whether I am on, or under the ground,
   The world cares little for me.

" The ways of men are busy and bright,
   And the voice of woman is kind ;
   'Tis sweet to the eyes to behold the light,
   But the dying and dead are blind.
   And the world goes round and round, etc.

" But if life awake and shall never cease
   On the future's distant shore,
   And the rose of love and the lily of peace
   Shall bloom there forever more ;

" Then let the world go round and round,
   And the sun sink into the sea ;
   For whether I am on, or under the ground,
   What does it matter to me !"

4. These studies really offer us the highest consolation in the presence of death, and the strongest

assurance of reunion and recognition in our hereafter.

> " Alas ! for him who never sees
> The stars shine through his cypress trees,
> Who hopeless lays his dead away,
> Nor waits to see the breaking day
> Across the mournful marbles play,
> Who hath not learned in hours of faith
> That truth, to flesh and sense unknown,
> That life is ever Lord of death,
> And love can never lose its own ! "

GREATER THINGS PROMISED TO FAITH.

"Thou shalt see greater things than these."--JOHN i. 50.

JESUS was one day walking, when He became conscious that two persons were following Him. Their names were Andrew and John. He turned and spoke to them. He asked them to go home with Him. It was not much of a home to ask anyone to—a rude hut on the banks of the Jordan. However, they accompanied Him there, and afterwards Andrew went and brought his brother Peter, and the three remained there with Jesus the rest of the afternoon, and probably slept there that night. But before they slept they knew and felt in their inmost hearts that the kingdom of heaven had come, that the hopes of long centuries were now fulfilled, and that they were in the presence of a priest holier than Aaron, of a prophet wiser than Moses, and of a king greater than David; and they participated in an event of the highest importance to all ages and races. This was the forming of the Christian Church, with three members, Andrew, Peter and John. Into what stately cathedrals that humble hut at Jordan has grown! Into what thronging multitudes of faithful disciples, and crowned martyrs, and kings, and learned men, the three fishermen have multiplied! Did ever a conversation among four men, for part of a day, seated on rude benches, throw such results up against the future? The next day Jesus started up the country to his old home in Galilee. He added on the way a man named Philip to his company, but Philip felt himself in such good company he would not go alone. He went after Nathanael, of whom we read in the Gospels as Bartholomew. Philip told him of this wonderful stranger, but he spoke of Him as "Jesus of Nazareth." Now, these were all Galilee men. Some business errand had taken them down into the vicinity of Jerusalem, perhaps to find market for their fish. Being Galilee men, they all understood what Nazareth meant. Nathanael was a man in higher circumstances and better bred than the rest, so that he was likely to be more unpleasantly affected than the others by anything from Nazareth. Hence his expression is contemptuous, "Can any good thing come out of Nazareth?" Still he walked along with Philip, and as they walked they came near enough to Jesus to hear Him say: "Behold an Israelite indeed, in whom is no guile!" And Nathanael knew perfectly well that these words were spoken concerning himself, for he was a very godly man, and must have known that he bore such a reputation; still he was surprised that Jesus knew anything about him, so he asked, "Whence knowest thou me?" Now, the answer to this

question was the stroke that won Nathanael's heart.
Mark its significance: " Before that Philip called
thee, when thou wast under the fig tree I saw thee."
Now, what was there in this to convince or win a
man ?   Why, it was a custom of the Jews to go
under the shade of the fig tree for secret prayer.
Nathanael had been thus engaged.   Like any good
man, he thought no one but himself knew anything
about his private devotions; but here, this man
Jesus shows that He knew about his most secret
prayers, and then the thought came that God alone
could have such knowledge.   This man must be
God.   He at once yielded up his whole heart, and
broke out, " Rabbi, thou art the Son of God, thou
art the King of Israel !"   It was a genuine conversion.

Nathanael believed on such evidence as could
reasonably be given, and Jesus commended him, and
promised that from that faith he should go on to
greater things.

From this we derive the principle : The faith that
accepts reasonable evidence shall be rewarded by
full revelations.

Nathanael had just one proof of the Deity of
Jesus, and he believed fully.   Then he received the
promise of greater things.

1. I notice this is a principle which applies in all
education.   A child believes the names of the letters
on his teacher's word.   He shall behold greater
things.   The boundless treasures of literature open

to him. Poetry, many-voiced, like a great choir and organ, pours upon his heart the full diapason of earthly melodies—the heart-psalm of all the ages! Philosophy lifts him into the spiritual realm of pure thought, entrancing as dream-land, yet as real as mountains and seas.

But suppose a child is a natural doubter, and he says he will not believe that this is A until you give him a proof of it which his reason can accept. And he wants you to demonstrate to him why Z is not called A, and A is not called Z, and he will believe nothing about it until you do so. It is plain he could not gain one step in advance. He would be forever shut out from the "greater things" contained in the world of literature.

When he comes to the study of history, if he will believe the general outlines, you promise him greater things. He shall descend into the minute details, and rise into the grand philosophical principles that are developed by history. He shall study the human race on a grand scale, and read lessons of profoundest wisdom for himself and for humanity, from the errors, and wrongs, and virtues of ages that are past and races that are no more.

And so in the study of every science. He must believe the first definitions. If he will not believe in the law of gravitation unless his eye can see it, then the great things of astronomy are forever shut out from his view. Yon twinkling stars, and revolving worlds, and blazing meteors, can be to him no more than the toys of a child. He can see no connection of vast systems, can realize no limitless expansion of the grand domain of life, can find no record of infinite wisdom in the harmony of a universe incomprehensibly great, nor trace the footsteps of the Deity walking everywhere in space unmeasured and inconceivable. These "greater things" can only be seen by one who will accept the preliminary principles.

Are we then to be surprised if in religious things all the great revelations are promised only to a faith that takes hold upon such evidence as is possible?

2. This principle applies to our confidence in Christianity as a system.

Nathanael began to believe on just one proof, that Jesus had divine knowledge. Let any man begin to believe in Christianity on such evidence as he can receive. There are the works of Jesus, His miracles. After ages of assault the Gospels yet remain without successful disputation, acknowledged as a correct record of the life and works of Jesus. All we have to do, therefore, is to decide if these were the works of a man, or if they must have been wrought by God. Was He who raised the dead, healed the sick, gave sight to the blind—above all, He who Himself arose from the dead—was He God or man? We have more than Nathanael had. The resurrection alone, which cannot be successfully disputed or explained away, is sufficient to lead those who, like Nathanael, are willing to believe on evidence, to surrender the whole heart to faith in Jesus. The scribes and Pharisees, who came asking a sign, had heard of the great works of Jesus. On that testimony, had they believed and followed Him, they should have themselves seen other and greater works. Instead of that, without any faith in their hearts at all, they came to Jesus asking such a sign as would suit their own ideas, and He gave them nothing.

But those who begin to believe on the testimony of His miracles shall see greater things in the way of evidence of the truth of Christianity itself. It is true that in our day we cannot see greater miracles of a material kind, "for since the blue heavens closed on the visions vouchsafed to St. Stephen and St. Paul, His earthly form has been visible no more." But there are moral miracles no less powerful for conviction. In 1 Cor. vi. 9, 10 and 11, we read : " Know ye not that the unrighteous shall not inherit the kingdom of God ? Be not deceived : neither fornicators, nor idolators, nor adulterers, nor effeminate, nor abusers of themselves with mankind, nor thieves, nor covetous, nor drunkards, nor revilers, nor extortioners shall inherit the kingdom of God. And such were some of you. But ye are washed, but ye are sanctified, but ye are justified in the name of the Lord Jesus, and by the Spirit of our God."

Now, this passage describes a moral miracle truly as wonderful as any material miracle ever witnessed

by living men. And such moral miracles we are witnessing all the time. All around us drunken men
become sober and continue so; vile men become pure
and live in chastity; dens of lust and debauchery
clean away their monstrous stench and wrong, and
become sweet and happy homes : the emblems of
obscenity and of universal degradation disappear
from a society thoroughly renovated. All these
things have we seen. We have seen atheists drop
their air of boastful defiance, and henceforth live as
believing Christians; we have seen pagans rise up
from the bondage of degrading superstitions, and
walking as happy saints of God. We have seen
great colossal amphitheatres that once reeked with
human blood, crumbling in ruins, while at their side
orphanages and homes for the aged and poor, and
hospitals for the sick, rise with a mission of perpetual mercy. To-day we see tenderness and love
spreading their mantle over the cell of the imprisoned
felon; we hear the tread of liberty as she goes forth
smiting and breaking forever the fetters of the slave;
and we see the schoolmaster taking the hand of the
ignorant, and philanthropy the hand of the poor;
and we see the sceptre passing from the hand of one
into the hands of many, and the multitude rules
itself, and the rich and the learned and the few no
longer go crashing over the poor, and the ignorant,
and the many, as though right was made to be their
exclusive sceptre and diadem. I say that in these
marvellous changes we have evidence of the vital,

heaven-given power of Christianity more convincing to the mind that is willing to accept reasonable evidence, than if our eyes actually beheld the dead raised to life again. All these things, and more, have been and are still being wrought by Christianity in lands both old and new. Let philosophy theorize and try to explain them by natural causes, but there they remain, and will remain, to confound scepticism, and to reassure the believing heart by growing up into the mighty culmination of evidence which unfolds the greater things to the eye sufficiently free from prejudice to behold them.

3. This principle applies to the pursuit of experimental religion, the knowledge of our salvation through Jesus Christ.

All men who believe that Christianity is from God cannot say that it makes them better men. All who believe in the Deity of Christ are not drawn by His love into a purer life, where they cease both to love what is sinful and to do it, which alone is the Christian salvation. This is because they are without any personal knowledge of Christ—they have no experience of His saving power.

Now, there are many things, any one of which may be sufficient to open the heart and to give to such a person a desire to be saved from the guilt of sin and from the love of it. It may be a fervent application of the truth from the pulpit. I was much struck with the words of an old man. We had been holding religious meetings for some days, and half a dozen earnest sermons had been preached, and this man said he had been examining his heart and applying the truths to himself, and he felt convinced that if he were not already converted he would not be able to resist the appeals that had been made. He felt that the arguments were convincing. Of course a good many did resist them, but the old man's words made me feel that the Word of God is sometimes used by Him in preaching to turn men to Himself. Or God may use the death of some one who has been greatly honored for many years, to lay upon the whole neighborhood the weight of a solemn injunction to awake and take hold upon the life of God. Or some great calamity may befall a people, and through the benumbing chill and darkness that hang upon every home, a voice louder than in whispers may be heard calling upon men to realize the possibilities of a nobler life. Or some long-slumbering promise made to a father or mother now in heaven may be mysteriously awakened into life and power, and may open upon the soul the windows of a new morning. Or a little child may have been taken, and the bright light shining along the way he has gone may reveal the hidden path to a nobler existence here and a grand immortality hereafter. If when the heart is thus made tender, the man would strive in the trembling steps of his feeble prayers to turn his face to Jesus, and to trust in Him, he should see greater things.

And there are many excellent men and women

against whom no word can be urged, who are thinking if only they do as well as they can they will
surely come out right. But their danger is, that
their religion has no Christ in it. Church, and service, and morality, but no Christ, no atonement for
their past sin! All around men tell what they
have found by trusting in Christ. Everyone can
receive such testimony for what it is worth. And
considering the kind of men who give it, it is certainly worth something. Now, if these people
would begin to trust in Christ on the strength of
this testimony, they would be led on to greater
things. We cannot make clear in words what they
would receive, but we can refer them to the sum-
mary of it. 1 Cor. ii. 9 : " Eye hath not seen, nor
ear heard, neither have entered into the heart of
man, the things which God hath prepared for them
that love Him." This is often understood to relate
to heaven, but if so, what mean the words that
immediately follow : " But the Lord hath revealed
them unto us by His Spirit ?" They are then given
to those taught of the Spirit in this world. They are
indeed the kingdom of Heaven ; but that part of it
which is possible to me is knowledge in this world,
for "the kingdom of God is not meat and drink ;
but righteousness, and peace, and joy in the Holy
Ghost." These greater things shall everyone see
who tries to believe.

And there are also men who are terribly immoral,
blasphemers and drunkards, and others. They see

their folly, and have tried to reform. They have
signed pledges and called their friends to witness.
They have kept them for a time and then failed.
There is no other way but to try the way of faith in
Jesus Christ.

There was a man who years ago had led a trusting woman to the altar, and vowed that he would
love and cherish her. And he meant it. He felt
her to be his crown and pride. He would have died
for her. But at length bad companions carried him
through the slides, and left him straggling with a
babe's strength against the awful current. Then he
would come home and curse and kick that woman
he promised to love. If anything crossed him without he would be more abusive to her. And she had
not seen from him one token of affection, or heard
a kind word from him for years. And her parents
were dead, and, as always in such cases, her friends
were few. One day this man attended a meeting,
where he was induced to sign the pledge. And
when he came in his first thought was, " How shall
I tell her. I fear she will faint away." He had·
many a time walked home intending to curse and
beat her, and never thought of her fainting! Well,
at last he got home and found her bent over a few
coals on the hearth. She did not look up as he
entered. He sat down and after a time he said:
" Mary." She did not turn or answer. Again he
said, " Mary," and received no answer. He felt
very uncomfortable. At last he broke out, " Mary,

I fear you are working too hard. You don't look so well as you used to. I am sure you are working a great deal too hard." Then she turned and looked at him, and said: "There is no help for it. There is nothing in the house to eat, and the children have had no supper." Feeling touched, he said: "Mary, I will help you after this." But she had no confidence, and though she did not understand his new turn, she said: "Little help I ever get from you." Then he burst out: "Mary, I have signed the pledge." And at this she rose up and went toward him, and she did faint; but his arms caught her, and his tears mingled with hers when she revived. One of the children who had never seen anything like this became alarmed and ran for her uncle, and as he came hurrying toward the house, he heard a great noise and feared the man was murdering his family. But when he entered both were on their knees and she was praying earnestly, "O God, strengthen poor Ned. O God, help him to keep his pledge. Let him never fall again." And at every petition he was crying out as loud as he could, "Amen, Amen." And this was the noise the uncle heard. And Ned and his wife kept on praying. They began their new life by believing that God alone could help and save them. And though they had very little at first, God certainly let them see greater things, for some years after when he told of this, he said, "Mary is alive and well and has some of her old happy look—like when we were married. Sometimes I
15

have been almost in the mouths of lions, but I have
been kept by prayer and have never fallen. Now
we have three good comfortable meals every day,
and we have good clothes for Sunday and all go to
church, and the children attend the Sunday School,
and I own the house where we live, and have a little
money in the savings bank." Did not God give
him to see greater things ?

4. I want to apply this principle to nations and
to churches. We are yet a young land. The jost-
ling tread of over-crowding millions breaks not yet
upon our confused ear. The glamour and pomp of
incalculable wealth dazzle not yet our imperfectly
educated senses. The thronging splendors of Old
World civilizations cast not yet their bright aurora
against our clear northern sky. And, like a boy
abashed in the presence of his big brother, we are
humble and silent before the great court of mighty
nationalities that circle round the earth : but the
eye that sees in the light of reasonable faith shall
yet see greater things for this young land. With
undisturbed feelings of admiration in which no envy
or jealousy mingles, I contemplate the truly wonderful cities of countless inhabitants and boundless
wealth that have sprung up both in the east and the
west of the United States, as if by the touch of the
wizard's wand. Well, we have as great possibilities, as
wide gates of opportunity opening before us, and as
fair a promise written against the sky of our future as
that land enjoyed a hundred years ago. Let then

our national faith wait and expand and grow, and
we ourselves when bent in age shall tread the
mighty thoroughfares of our eastern cities, when
hurrying hundreds of thousands shall wage the conflicts of peace in commerce and manufacture; and
in this grèat North-west our children shall forget
the points which their fathers marked as centres, so
completely shall they be overflown by the insweep-
ing tide of population and of commerce. No shadow
of doubt darkens my faith in the future of this city
and this land, guarded and consecrated by the
watchful eye of the northern stars. If there were
no fluctuations, there would be no waves. Depressed to-day, we rise on the foaming crest to-
morrow. Let us go on in confidence. We may
make of this land what we will. This city gives
promise that it, too, will be a city of churches. If
we hand down to the next generation all the sacred
traditions and all the hallowed memories of a
church-going, Bible-reading, Sabbath-observing,
God-fearing people, no shock that at any time may
break upon our frontier from the atheism and com-
munism and anarchy of foreign shores, shall ever
tear this land out of God's right hand. God has
honored our Church by letting us place before
Christendom the astonishing example of men rising
above prejudices and traditions to join hands in
working for God alone. I feel my little world enlarged by this touch of God's favoring mercy.
There have before been unions of different churches,

but four different bodies coming in on one platform
is something new. I take it as a promise that a
weapon of wider influence shall be given into our
hand.

In educational work, in the use of the press, in
promoting and sustaining missions, the Church will
enjoy a vantage ground never before reached.

As to this "Grace Church," we are now seeing the
greater things promised to the faith of men who
began the work of Methodist missions here years
ago. And yet greater things are possible. The
conversion of one sinner this day would be a greater
result than over-crowded congregations or large
collections. A revival of religion that shall move
men all along the line, and quicken into goodness all
there is in us, and bring scores and hundreds from
worldliness and sin, would be a crowning blessing,
in comparison with which all the grandeur or im-
pressiveness of this material temple would sink into
insignificance. If we begin and continue our work
in faith these greater things will come.

SELF-DENIAL.

"If any man will come after Me, let him deny himself and take up his cross and follow Me."—MATT. xvi. 24.

IN the life of Jesus the dark shadow of the closing tragedy fell all along His path. When He spoke these words the cross was not far away. Already His mind was being penetrated with its gloom, as one shivers in anticipation of the chilling air of the evening. But that was *His* cross. In His thought, however, Himself and His followers were never widely separated. And nearness to that darkest passage in His own life awakened His tenderest sympathies for His people in view of what they must likewise suffer. They were destined to share His glory, but they should reach it through the dark passage-way of tears and sufferings; and not until they could in some measure enter into the fellowship of His deep unspoken anguish of spirit because of sin, and the burden it had laid upon His own soul. They must bear a cross as well as He.

It is our privilege to follow them as well as Him along the tear-dewed path marked with drops of blood through which they reached the gates of glory.

Paul lets us know the deep secrets of his own life. Beaten with stripes, stoned, in prisons, in dangers by land and sea, the alienation of best friends, the misjudgment of the truest motives, all the way his day of life a day of storm, until the night falls and he is hurried headless out into the silence! And much the same was the experience of the other apostles and of men and women little less worthy, joining hands down the Christian ages, until even at our feet fall the shadows of the last of the martyrs for the cross. To maintain a Christian profession has been in the past to be exposed to danger, to loss, to reproach, and even to death. Christ said, " In the world ye shall have tribulation." Then He added : " Be of good cheer, I have overcome the world." It is our happiness to live in a time when that language has a new meaning. He has held the hands of His people through ages of storm, until now over the world, as over the Sea of Galilee, His voice is heard, " Peace be still," and the winds and the waves of violence obey His power. His spirit has so far prevailed among men that His people scarcely know any more what violent persecutions for His name mean.

But because of this great privilege of hearing His name and allying with His cause in peace, there is a great mistake into which people are constantly falling, that is, the mistake of supposing His teaching so liberal that it will lay no restraints upon human nature. Because men do not tear and

destroy each other on account of the religious faith,
many seem to think that the great laws that govern
human nature now run exactly parallel with the
great principles that pervade the teaching of Christ's
gospel, instead of meeting like two violent currents
in opposite directions and cutting through each other,
as they always have done, and as, in fact, they do
yet. As the result of this error, you find churches
to-day whose standard of morality and religious
development will lead them to admit everybody to
fellowship who is good enough to escape the
hands of the police, and who judge of development in Christian grace by the readiness with which
a person adapts himself to the rules of politeness
recognized in an ever-changing society. It is the
effort of the world to declare that human nature is
good without the Spirit of God, that it needs no
regeneration, that man is saved by external surface
culture. The fact is the world is so far affected by
the spirit of Christ that it wants to be religious,
but is not enough affected by it to be willing to pay
the price of any very great sacrifice for religion. Such
a temper of mind can only be satisfied by saying that
human nature needs no watching, no restraining.

But on the very lowest ground we can take, either
there must be some self-denial—a cross in some
form, or no religion. The lowest ground we can
take is that the Christian religion is simply one
among a number of means of cultivating human
nature. On this ground we need never mention

atonement, regeneration, repentance, restitution,
future punishment, nor anything that is humbling
to the human heart, and that is calculated to remind
man of his sins. He may hold his head aloft in a
pride that even Lucifer could not surpass. His
religion ranks with the high school, the Lyceum
and the art gallery, as a means of refining him.
You cannot put religion lower than that if you
allow it a name at all.

But can you get along even on that plane without
any self-denial? Do men enjoy the benefit of any
means of culture—even the lowest—without self-
denial? Can the boy derive any good results from
school and college without self-denial? Will he
not sit many an hour at his desk when mountain,
field and stream tempt him to wander, sail and
swim? Will he not again and again forego the
pleasures of appetite that his mind may be more
clear for the great problems before him? And who
ever gained the prize in a school of art without
such self-denial as sometimes almost bends the head
to the earth? One evening last week, with a good
many of you, I watched the movement of a distinguished pianist's fingers. So easy it was in appearance, it seemed that any child might do it, yet in
fact was so difficult of attaining that a life might be
worn out without reaching it. Whence come the
sculpture and painting that the infinite genius of
Italy has inspired with breathing life! Behold this
masterpiece, the Crucifixion, on the walls of a great

church! Young Murillo enters and fixes his eyes
upon it. He moves not, nor turns away. The
hours pass. Evening comes, and the old verger lays
his hand on Murillo's shoulder and asks, "For what
do you wait?" Without removing his eyes the
rapt youth replies, "Until Joseph comes to take Him
down from the cross, and the women to anoint Him
for the burial."

They who gave the marble a shape so true to
nature that you can almost feel that it is your
brother, and put upon the canvas forms that almost
speak and answer back your smile, reached the lofty
eminence of infinite genius by infinite toil and
patience. As to self-denial, many of them could not
purchase a fashionable garment for themselves, so
completely had they forgotten such indulgence.
Their neglected appetites would turn from an epi-
cure's treat as from a stranger. They taught their
bodies that sleep was not an indulgence but a necessary relief from toil—little better in its character
than theft. Why, now, if religion is going to cultivate a man's nature, can he expect it to enjoin no
self-denial?

But leave religion out of the question. How many
people are there who can live without denying
themselves something? In a mansion so grand that
money can bring nothing more into it, amid doctors
and nurses the rich mother will neither sleep nor
eat because of her sick child. Families by the
thousand are going without some little gratifications

every day that they may be able to have some
greater good a summer holiday, some coveted
article of household ornament or utility. In fact,
human life without self-denial in some form is impossible. Men and women are everywhere denying
themselves a lower that they may gain a higher
good.

When, then, we consider that everywhere in life
there is self-denial, and that by every variety of
culture men try to raise either mind or body to
a nobler character; that when the student would
make the most of his intellect, and when the cham-
pion would fit his body for the noblest work in a
race, the object can only be gained by rigorous self-
denial, it does reflect the meanness of human nature
that people will bear the Christian name and yet be
unwilling to make any self-denial for Christ's sake.
Are not people thus unwilling? Let me ask what
can you recall that you have denied yourself for
His name? As I ask the question, certain forms of
sin, to which in your secret heart you feel a strong
tendency, arise in your thought, and you say to
your conscience, I have given up these for Christ's
sake. Let me ask you to look again, and you will
find that you have denied yourself a good many of
these for fear of going to jail, and a good many
others through fear of being lashed by the scandal-
loving tongue of general society. Many of you are
compelled to acknowledge to your conscience that
for Christ's sake you have denied yourself nothing

—you have let human nature have its way because it was pleasant to do so, only restraining it where it was likely to bring you into conflict with the law.

Now, we must say that the respectability which keeps a person out of jail is something less than the religion of Christ. A little while ago I said that in the very lowest idea men can have of Christianity, it requires self-denial and a cross. We must raise it immeasurably above that lowest idea of it.

There will always be

1. The cross of doctrine. Human guilt is not a pleasant doctrine to proud spirits. Repentance is full of offence, and restitution is intolerable. A just law from God, which inflicts just punishments, is hideous to human nature. Atonement and pardon, the taking man to heaven as a pauper, letting him pay nothing as a purchase price, stings the haughty spirit. Yet these truths must always bend the necks of those who enter heaven. Men say, make the Church and Christianity liberal. But in some respects Christianity, when true to its mission, must always seem to some illiberal. It can never be liberal towards sin, or any impurity, howsoever refined in outward appearance. It can never be liberal by forgetting its Christ. Yet here is where the worldly man wants liberality. The cross of doctrine must always remain.

2. There is the cross of sacrifice for the Christian's own benefit and purity. It is in kind the same as the self-denial we have already noticed in the

student and the artist. It is the sacrifice of pleasure of the body for the sake of purity of conscience.
Every Christian man in the world must practise this
self-senial by contenting himself with less money
than he could have by adopting the world's ways.
Men and women must be content with less of
worldly pleasure. This is the difficult turn in the
road. I cannot deny that the question of amusements has difficulties. Take some games that are
played in fashionable life, the theatre, the dance,
the races, no matter of what kind. Now, I could
not say that the person who indulges in any or in
all of these must necessarily be eternally lost. I do
not put the argument on that ground. Indeed, I
cannot decide just how far such amusements may
be consistent with some degree of religious life, and
with the spirit of Christ: but from everything we
can learn it does seem that a great love for such
things reveals a low grade of spiritual life, and little
sensibility to the strong claims of Christ. The love
of such amusements is one of the things that one
may easily deny himself for Christ's sake, and I am
persuaded that anyone who would take upon himself the cross of such a sacrifice, who would freely
give up everything of this nature that lies upon
doubtful ground, would be a thousand times repaid
in his own spiritual development, in his sense of
moral security and freedom from uncomfortable
questionings of conscience. But the prevalent idea
of religion is not self-conquest and elevation of char-

acter by aspirations after the heavenly; but rather a respectable gilding for the pleasures of fashionable life. Such a spirit that yields nothing for Christ may have a church, but it is not religion. The religion of Christ as taught in the New Testament is a spirit of self-sacrifice.

About forty years ago a young lady of New York, after contending against tremendous difficulty and opposition, found herself at last an object of great admiration and envy on account of her poetical and other imaginative writings. She had won a crown. She might do what she would. Fanny Forrester was a person the highest in the land would gladly court. But almost immediately after her triumph was universally acknowledged, it became known that this favorite had consented to become the wife of Adoniram Judson, then about 58 years of age, whom death had already parted from two devoted wives, and to go with him into the heart of the darkest heathenism to burn out her life-lamp in a struggle with a barbarous language, a cruel race, and a climate full of pestilence, all for love of the Lord Jesus Christ and those for whom He died. The fashionable world was confounded then as it is now when one casts down its crown for the sake of a crown of eternal life. In well-dressed and polite circles it was passed around, " The woman is mad." So people whose hearts know nothing of the love of Christ always think when one chooses Christ before the world, that is to them their all. But this woman knew herself and her choice well. She took up this cry and wrote and published a grand essay on "The Madness of the Missionary Enterprise," in which she fully exposed the selfishness and hollowness of the money-making, pleasure-loving world of her own people. She cleared herself and her cause and left the imputation of madness on the other side. If you had her gifts would you make any such sacrifice? Do you make anything like it now, proportionate to your gifts and opportunities? Yet, suppose you won the brightest crown possible, who is wiser, she or you? In 1821 Napoleon died at St. Helena, crying " Tête d'Armée." They were his last words inspired by clangor of his rushing life. Twenty-four years afterwards a ship anchored in a port of the same island. In the cabin of that ship lay the second Mrs. Judson, ill, returning from her finished work. Her final words were, " I ever love the Lord Jesus Christ," and then she sank into a quiet slumber of an hour, and awoke with the angels. France was proud to honor Napoleon's remains. The missionary's grave was marked by a simple slab, bearing her name, age, date of death, and the verse,

" Sweetly she sleeps here on this rock of the ocean,
 Away from the home of her youth,
And far from the land where with heartfelt devotion,
 She scattered the bright beams of truth."

Which from St. Helena found the brighter crown, the Emperor, or she who denied herself for Christ?

A crown and triumph worthy the name can only be gained by a life of religious self-denial. I have read that an ancient senator told his son of the great honors about to be conferred on certain citizens whose names were in a book he held in his hands. The son desired the names ; but the father would only tell him that they were such as had performed noble deeds and rendered great services to the State. Hitherto, the son had been a careless libertine and a great drunkard ; but now he put himself into retirement, repented of his past sins, subdued his passions, and when the next time brave men were honored, and soldiers came forward for their wreaths, he also came to claim one for himself. He said, "If honors be given to conquerors, I have gained the noblest conquest of all. These men have subdued stronger foes, but I have conquered myself." There is another book in which the names are written of those who are chosen for high honors—it is the Book of Life, but none are written there but such as have conquered themselves. The self-loving and ease-seeking, who despise any sacrifice of what their flesh likes, are not the ones chosen for high honors.

A woman had a pleasant home near Cleveland, Ohio. Men were talking of choosing her husband as a candidate for the presidency of the United States. She asked Governor Jewell, an intimate friend, if it would pay to leave their pleasant home. The Governor replied, "Yes; in a year your husband will be President of this country, and hold the highest office on the globe." The months hurried by ; a funeral train was carrying Mrs. Garfield back to the pleasant home. She sent for Governor Jewell, and asked him, " Has it paid ?" He replied, " Yes : for that man is the best loved man on the globe." So much sacrifice for so much love ! No self-denial, no cross, no laying down and emptying out of self—no love ! How shall it be with us when death comes forcibly to empty us out ?

WINNING SOULS.

"He that winneth souls is wise."—PROVERBS xi. 30.

THIS is certainly true, for if he were not wise he could not do it. As a rule, just the hardest thing to do with a man is to win his soul. Now, if the object were to win his *money*, that work would not call forth any very great skill. Not long since, in an old newspaper, I read an elaborate article on the game of poker. It explained the various tricks employed by old players to compel the game to favor their hand whether strong or weak. I could see nothing in the whole practice worthy the name of wisdom. Low cunning best describes the directing genius in all the arts and tricks of play whereby men's money is won. Yes, it is easy to win men's money. Advertise, in striking form, a lottery, the veriest swindle, or some patent nostrum—sure cure for everything—and men will just pour their gold into the hand of the manipulator.

So, also, it is comparatively easy to win men's friendship. If your position in the world is higher than theirs, notice them, patronize them; if lower, flatter them. You will so bind them to your carriage wheel. Or buy your goods of them—you

16

will rivet their souls to yours in abiding friendship
until it suits your convenience or interest to buy of
someone else. Or vote for a man, or for his candidate—a fellow-feeling is at once established, and he
will be your firm, true friend until the next day.
Treat him with all neighborly kindness, help him or
his family, and, if he is worth owning as a friend,
you will have his heart. Still no great wisdom is
called to the front.

So, too, no great tax will be laid upon your powers
to gain a man's influence. If you want to sell something you will easily procure any number of valuable
testimonials asserting its usefulness and unparal-
leled excellence. No small matter is more surprising than the ease with which testimonials and
assurances may be procured, even from men in the
most distinguished positions. No tax is laid upon
wisdom in getting the benefit of other men's influence. Indeed, it is often unnecessary even to be-
have yourself with particular care. And if you
cannot secure it in any other way you can generally
buy it : and whatever can be bought for money is,
of all good things, most easily attained.

So much, then, and even more, you may win from
a man without being particularly wise ; but if you
would win his soul you must at once rise to a higher
plane of action ; and develop superior skill in
adapting your means to the end which you contemplate.

The first tax laid upon you is to get the man's

attention. You approach him about his soul. He does not quite comprehend what you mean. It is true that the word soul is in his vocabulary, because away back in the far-off years his mother taught him to pray when his heart was tender, and his whole nature was like a hot-bed for moral truths. But since then mists have settled over the shores of his sea. He knows of a certainty that he is just now in storm and conflict, trying to do the best for himself and others: but he is not quite sure that there is any landing. It seems to him very likely that the voyage will end by his just sinking out of sight, and there will be no more of him. But you speak to him of his soul, and of the shining shore. The shore he cannot see, and the soul never shows itself. He never comes upon it in any inventory of his effects. It is not anything that he can put upon the market. As to his body, if he pricks it, it will bleed. If he allows it to get chilly, it will turn blue. This soul, which you would set him to seek for, never manifests itself in any such way. It never comes out before him and says, "I am hungry. I am cold, or lonely." He cannot easily understand why you should come to him about it. If you made some proposal about his house, or his prairie lands, or his factory, or stocks, he would understand you. But to exercise your zeal and anxiety about him, and yet not want to sell him anything, nor to buy, nor to get a subscription, he naturally feels that it would be as well for you to promptly explain.

Week before last I was in conversation with a Provincial Chief Justice. He spoke of some acquaintances of a former day who sent word to him in advance of their arrival in his town that they desired to see him. He was busy, and so left a check with a friend who was to meet them in his name. Said he, " The friend returned the check much to my surprise, for I have found that the first and bottom plank in the platform of such people is that they want money." Now, this idea is so common that when you approach a man not desiring to make anything out of him, his eyes become bleared by the spectacle. He will either regard you with suspicion, or else he will think you are trifling, and set you down as a fool. Now, what room there is for the highest skill—what exquisitely delicate movement is necessary—to first awaken a man to as clear a consciousness that he has a soul to save, as he has of the existence of his store, or bank, or goods lying at the depot to be moved into his warehouse. With how many of us who sit here the obligation to save the soul is much less distinct than the mortgage to raise, or the bill to meet!

But suppose you are wise enough by admirable tact and address to gain his attention, to arouse an interest in him, to get him to think about his soul and its salvation, to realize its existence, its immortality, and its dangers ; then, shall I say, your difficulty is but well begun. He and you will alike realize how completely it is shut in by adverse influences.

There is his business. It may be bad in its very motive. There is the liquor traffic. It is granted that the men engaged in it have no worse motive than other men. They desire wealth for themselves and their families, but it is a trade in which money can be made rapidly and easily, and a man soon gets hardened down to it. Or take the speculator, whose business is simply one mode of gambling. Or take the undisguised professional gambler. If you succeed in awakening in any of these an interest in his soul, what can he do ? Years in such a manner of life have disqualified him for any regular pursuits. He could not earn a living if he gave up his present course in life. Then such a one has no proper idea of the value of money. He has been in the habit of getting it easily. He is reckless in its use. He could not live upon what would be a good income for another man. The fact is the devil has his soul mortgaged to a damning business ! But leave such pursuits, come up to the plane of honorable occupations. Many men have decidedly bad methods of conducting a good enterprise. They are closely connected with others, influential in their calling, who say that honesty in trade is impossible. When such a one is awakened to a desire to save his soul he sees that to do it he must rise to a higher discrimination between right and wrong than most men have with whom he deals, and by so much he will be a loser. And not only so, his connection with men in business almost forces him down to

their level when out of business. He must drink
with them, and play with them, and go to their club,
and neglect his home, and so he gets fairly started
on the road to dissipation. Of his own desire he
never would have got into any such ways. Then in
addition to all this his social life comes in. The
influence of men's words and acts and pervading
example all day is not all. Going home, where he
ought to find rest and influences pushing him upward and to better things, his wife and daughters
set the full cup before him again. On his own
carpet and at his own table the suggestion to his
thoughts of evil goes on. He is not an Ariel that
no thought of rebellion against moral restraints
can ever enter his mind. Evil thoughts do come
in over the choicest service of silver, amid the
most brilliant glare, and even the richest adorn-
ments. Now, the man is awakened to feel an
interest in his soul's salvation. How can he
escape from all these hindrances? Considering how
rapidly the evil grows and hardens into confirmed
habit, there is little chance of getting his soul out
of its imprisonment. Trench after trench is dug
around it. Not one band but a thousand are upon
it. What wisdom is needful to induce him to try
to get away!

Some say there is no personal devil. Well, if
there is not, certainly the chances and accidents
have made the conditions of life exactly what a
creature such as we think the devil would be

would have made them. If there is no devil, then there ought to be, because the condition of this world is perfectly adapted to his desires. It is a great pity that someone should not enjoy it. When the awakening man finds how his soul is shut in, it will be hard for him to understand it without feeling that some malignant monster has deeply planned his destruction!

But these are not all the difficulties. Give him to understand his duty to his soul, and get aroused to the point of determining to be free or to die. Then for the first time he detects that years of neglect have depraved his tastes, destroyed his sensibility. He has been a slave so long, that now when the proclamation of liberty is made he is afraid to leave the old plantation. He must return there to sleep at night. A few years ago (February, 1882), I made a visit to the penitentiary at Kingston. While speaking to the warden at the entrance gate, a man passed out carrying a small satchel. I was told that he had just been dismissed, after serving a term of three years. I could not conceal my interest in him. My eye followed him as he walked up the gentle slope pointing directly towards the town. What must a man's feelings be to find himself free, after being treated like a dumb brute for three years! Constantly under lock and key, watched by keepers, and led out to work and then led back to the stall again, his food thrown to him as if to a horse in the manger! Three years of such a life,

but now he is free! He can go where, and do just
what he will. He is dependent on his own exer-
tions. I felt strangely fascinated with this released
criminal. I said to the warden, " What will he do ?
Where will he go ? " " Oh," he replied carelessly,
" he will soon be back here." (This was his second
term—two years the first time.) " No one wants to
employ a man just out of penitentiary. The world
is rough on them; and then, anyway, they have
learned so to depend upon others that they cannot
take care of themselves." And just in the same
way the soul is disrobed of its royalty and manhood
so that it cannot keep up an even desire after a
better life and a brighter world. A former pastor
of this church, now deceased, in some interesting
sketches of travel, describes the Digger Indians of
the Pacific coast. It seems that at certain seasons
they actually diet on grass. A chieftain was captured by United States soldiers. Fed on their rations
he pined away. He kept saying when food was
offered to him that it was the season for grass.
Well, at last they let him out upon the grass, and
he very soon had fully recovered his tone. His
natural appetite had become so depraved that he
would have starved on luxuries, his nature was
incapable of enjoying, while he could live and
flourish in a beast's manner of life. The same is
true of the mind. The average intellect is allowed
to drop to the level of the daily newspaper. It is
really unable to enjoy anything but the listless

roaming from item to item, skipping every elaborate
article. That morning dish of hash—the newspaper
—disqualifies the intellect of scores and scores for
poetry, philosophy, science and religion, which they
were made to enjoy, and upon which the intellect
should feed, only reverting to the newspaper with
its five-line items as to a drive for recreation. As
the mind and body, so the soul is degraded by the
treatment it receives. As the loss of appetite
means loss of health, a decline in vital energy—the
beginning of death—so the loss of desire for religious
duty means the beginning of death to the soul. It
is incapable of finding its ecstasy in God. It is so
depraved that it is fully satisfied with sin.

Another test of the wisdom of the soul-winner is
the fact that the man can only come out of this condition of slavery and debasement by an act of his
own. It can only be by a strong decision of his
own will. But he has been insensibly taught to
regard such an act as a weakness. He has heard
men speak patronizingly, and more than half-pity-
ingly, of one who has turned to give serious attention to the salvation of his soul. Others, again,
have treated such concern with undisguised ridicule
and contempt. The impression made upon his
mind by such words has been deepening for years,
and you are to produce upon his mind an impression so strong that he will rise up determined to
perform that very act, so lightly spoken of, or die.
Persuade waters to flow up the hills. Teach wild

beasts not to relish the flesh of domestic animals. Show a man how to hate the city where he was born and has spent all his years, and which he has seen doubling its population and wealth two or three times. The work is no greater than that set before you in winning a soul from the world.

Then the tax on your wisdom is the heavier in that the soul is to be won, not bought. If it were a purchase, that would be the subject merely of a simple calculation. In these days of great accumulation, an humble man might set before him as his aim the purchase of the Bank of Montreal. We could easily make the calculation presenting to his eye just what he must do. Greater things have been undertaken and accomplished by an individual. Set the soul's value high as you choose, if it were possible, a man might plan to purchase it and succeed. But it is not to be taken in this way. The nearest we can come to it is that if a man gains the whole world, but in doing so loses his own soul, he makes a bad bargain. One cent comes as near to its value as hundreds of millions. It is not to be bought. It has been bought already by the precious blood of Christ.

Nor yet is it to be captured, like an enemy to society. As it has been bought, so has it been captured (2 Timothy ii. 26). The infatuation under which it is held, as already described, illustrates the thorough capture of it. The fact is that *Christ has bought and owns the soul; the devil has captured*

and holds it. The wise man must go and stand
between Christ and the devil, and win the soul back
to God. As Christ is man's advocate with God, so
the soul-winner is under the blessed Spirit, God's
advocate with man.

Now, there are two senses in which things are
won. There is the case where one wins at play.
The stake is entirely passive, unconscious, and un-
interested. The Church and godly men and the
Holy Spirit are playing a game with the devil in
which the stake is the human soul. Indeed, we
may say that every man is playing such a game
with the devil for his own soul. I remember an
impressive picture whose weird effect easily returns
to me when I think upon it. It represented a man
and the devil seated at the table playing this terrible game. The game was chess. The stake the
man's soul. The man has made bad play. His
pawns were marked " honesty," " truth," " purity,"
sensibility," and so on. They were all taken by the
devil. " Hope," his king, is being fast closed around.
It is plain that the man has already lost the game.
With consummate skill the artist had thrown into
the picture the devil's sense of power over his vic-
tim, and the man's slowly dawning consciousness of
irrevocable misfortune, as his hope is cut off. How
many are playing that desperate game! Virtue is
gone. Honor is lost. Reputation is ruined. Hope
lives yet, but it will soon go. Then the man is lost.
Then the devil will drag the shivering soul away
with him to hell.

But there is another sense in which men may win
-not as one wins in play, but as a suitor wins the
heart of another. In this case the object of pursuit
is one party to the contest. It is in this sense the
soul-winner must gain the soul. Now, we have
already seen what is necessary in this pursuit. The
soul must be awakened to its own value and danger.
Then desire and aspiration must be enkindled in it.
How difficult it is to quicken any hopefulness in
one long subject to rebuffs, privation and hardship,
or in one who has never had any experience of
success! Take a schoolboy who never was ahead
of his class; a pastor who never sees any growth
in his congregation, or any souls converted. How
hard for such to look with any animation toward
the future! So it is with much difficulty that
an unsaved man can be made to believe the possibilities of happiness and power that are before
him in the spiritual life. Another thing necessary
is to instruct the soul as to its duty and privilege
and responsibility.

When this awakening is complete there yet remains the furnishing of native power. The man
must move himself in the matter. But he cannot
be moved without power. What motives will raise
him and cause him to start? You would say that
is easy. Are not heaven and hell before him? Yes;
but how much motive power do these facts furnish
to the average man of the world? They have heard
of them all their lives. It is like coming to one who

has passed his days and raised his family in the east, and trying in his old age to draw him off to the distant west by telling him of its charms and advantageous openings for a new beginner. He has been hearing and resisting these arguments all his days.

Is it likely that they will prevail upon him now? It is like telling one who never cared for an orchestra and chorus, of the power of music, and so trying to induce him to learn to sing. No; though heaven and hell are great motives, men are familiar with them, and are in the habit of trifling with them. They will not alone be sufficient to move a man from his indifference and slumber. The prospect of heaven is not a sufficient motive to a man until he gets some of heaven in himself. Then it will move him. Before that it is like beauty to a blind man, or melody to the deaf.

What can the soul-winner do for his motive? He must depend upon the aid and power of the Divine Spirit to provide a motive which no one can see, which even the person who is moved by it does not understand. Were it not for this power no soul would ever be won. The difficulties are insuperable to human skill and argument.

Next, the soul-winner must be himself a motive, so far as human agency can provide any power. This is only doing in religion what men do in everything else. One man is a motive power to another often in business. A man would sink but for the strength begotten into him by his friend, not merely

by helping him with money, but by inspiring him
with confidence. So in society matters, one strong
woman will lead and control a score by her single
motive power. A bad man sometimes fastens upon
a youth to lead him into vicious ways—to betray
him into some den of vice, or to teach him the
gambler's act. The youth is not easily destroyed;
but he is not left to himself for a day until the end
is gained, and he loves iniquity for its own sake,
and thanks his own destroyer. Now, if in the common business of life, and even for infamous purposes one man may become a motive to another,
why may not the soul-winner also support by his
magnetism and presence and power the weak when
he first begins to reach up after good? There are
many who never will be, never can be, saved until
some other person thus devotes himself to redeem
their lives! I know there are many hypocritical
people who have a great concern lest anyone should
enter upon a religious life through the too persuasive influence of another. But they would drag
a man off, tie him up in a bag, or get him drunk to
secure his vote. They would let a vile man drag
another down to perdition without a word. But when
you come to grasp a man out of the fire, "Oh!"
they cry out, "that is enthusiasm!" Away
with such vile hypocrisy! Let us be as wise to save
the lost as men are in worldly affairs. I shall not
forget the words of a business man to me once. His
work was carried on by a personal canvass. He

spoke of a certain prominent business man, and said that he had made an earnest effort to establish business relations with him. The man was gruff, almost rude, and said he, " I gave him up—something I have since learned not to do with any man." It struck my mind very forcibly.

THE PHARISEE AND PUBLICAN.

"God be merciful to me a sinner."—LUKE xviii. 13.

THE narrative from which the text is taken
brings before us two men. They were very
unlike. They differed greatly in what each thought
of himself. They differed just as much in their re-
spective opinions of each other.

One of these men was a Pharisee. He belonged
to that largest sect among the Jews, the members of
which prided themselves upon the strictness with
which they observed all the outward forms of
religion.

They furnish a good illustration of men's tendency to lose the substance while clinging to the form.
In the great Roman Catholic churches of Montreal,
the priests sometimes carry a vase in which is a
bright flame that shines through the porcelain, and
this flame is constantly burning incense that spreads
its perfume through all the surrounding air. But
sometimes while the priest swings his vase the flame
within goes out. No incense is burnt after that; it
gives forth no fragrance : but flame and incense have
no weight, and the man keeps on swinging his vase
aloft, while no glowing light shines through, and no

sweet perfume is given forth. Now, that vase represents some Christian people who keep strictly to all the forms of religion when their life has ceased to give out any of the influence of the Christian spirit, and their hearts no longer glow with its light. This was true of the Pharisees in our Saviour's time. Having been a holy, separate people in their origin, they had lost all the glow of the inner light, and retained only the empty frame of forms and ceremonies.

The other man whom the narrative brings before us was a publican. He belonged to a class universally noted and despised beyond any people in the world. As tax-gatherers, their whole course was an uninterrupted career of extortion and oppression. Hence, they could not but be despised.

Now, we find these two men in the temple at the hour of prayer on the same day. The church is a good place in which to study men, because, then, people are likely to be honest; though, of course, if one goes to church as he goes to a concert, or to the theatre, or to a ball, merely to see, to be seen and amused, he will probably carry there the same airs of dissimulation which he practises in any place of social concourse. But if, like these two men, he feels some sense of God's greatness, and some desire to worship Him, he will cast aside all efforts to appear in any way different from what he is.

Let us begin with the Pharisee. He stood and prayed, "God, I thank thee." Now, that is good. I

17

am glad to make the acquaintance of such a man as that. He seems to be a perfect gentleman. Oh, it is well for us when we can so far enter the temple, like this Pharisee, that the heart is full and glowing with grateful feelings, and they rise to our lips before any other. We have been kept alive through another week of dangers. Providential mercies have filled our hands. Some great blessing has come to our family, some deliverance from calamity ; or the toil and anxiety of business have not broken down the happiness of home, and there has been some return for toil; some entanglements that threatened badly have straightened themselves all out, or a boy that gave his parents some anxiety for his future has entered a good situation and is doing well —when anything of this kind is uppermost in the mind, as one enters the temple and swells the first note of thanksgiving, it is well. He will have a good time in the sanctuary on that day. The service will not be tedious—the day not long !

So this Pharisee seems to have come. "God, I thank thee . . . that I am not as other men." Ah ! that is bad ! After all, I feel anxious about this man. It shows a bad vein in his character to begin so soon to compare himself with others. We could overlook it if a man's first thought in church was, " I thank God that this autumn day my fields are golden with a rich harvest of waving grain—the ripened wheat is ready for the sickle," though we might think that some other things ought to have

swelled the first note of thanksgiving! If he began,
" I thank God that business is improving; last week
a bad debt was paid that has enabled me to meet a
large note that was troubling me," we would think
that some selfishness had crept into his praise, but we
would excuse it. But no man would have a thought
of selfishness if he began, "I thank God that during
the last week my little child has recovered from a
distressing and dangerous illness;" or, when the affliction had been long continued and very painful, and
had grown hopeless, if he should break out in thanks
while the tears would fall like rain, that the end
had come to the long sacrament of pain and anguish
—" the child is at rest, and now, while I lift my heart
in praise here, the little voice is joining in the choir
invisible—he meets to worship with the angels."
No, there would be no selfishness in such thanksgiving as that! And there are many things that
may properly enough swell the first note of thanksgiving; but when, of them all, a man must turn to
that one thing that he is not like others, it looks
badly, and you may well feel some concern about
that man! Of course, there are some respects in
which it is perfectly true that one person is not like
others, and for that fact most persons may well feel
a reasonable amount of gratitude; but those differences between one and others are not likely to come
first to the mind of a genuine worshipper. Such a
one will think of himself in that character in which
in God's house all are equal. The Duke of Welling-

ton once knelt at the altar to receive the sacrament of the Lord's Supper. Then there came and
knelt at his side, a plain, poorly-dressed working
man. One of the attendants was about to remove
the latter; but the Duke turned, and—I do not
think it was an interruption to his devotions to say
such a thing—he said, "No, we all are equal here."
All the distinctions made for social or politic reasons
in the outside world are entirely without authority
here. In the temple a man has no right even to
know that he is not as others are.

But our concern deepens about this Pharisee, for
he is not only self-righteous, but meanly invidious.
He thanks God that he is not as other men, but
points out and mentions one particular person, "even
as this publican." Now, that was not in his ritual.
I suppose he raised his eyes for the moment, and as
he did so, saw this man. He looked hard! How
could it be otherwise? Let any person enter a
business in which he must be constantly stultifying
his conscience by the basest reasons and most paltry
arguments; let him keep doing what his better sense
tells him to be wrong, and every day justifying himself by such subterfuge as, "If I don't do it, some
one else will," or "I must live," or "You see, I have
a family to support," and in a short time such a
course will make his heart hard, his conscience will
come to be as if seared with a hot iron, and he will
appear hard in gait and in expression. Then the
manner in which he was always treated in perform-

ing his duties would make him awkward and rude
and coarse, even if his work had been strictly right
and good. No doubt he was dressed badly and
seemed strange in the place, for it is not at all likely
that he went to the temple very often. The Pharisee
took all this in at a glance, and he no doubt pitied
him somewhat and despised him a great deal. I
think he felt toward him very much as sometimes
you have felt when some wayfarer has made his
way into your church, who looked rough and hard
and poor ; his face was bloated, and his eyes blood-
shot, and his bruised countenance showed marks of
violence. Some good impulse led him into the
consecrated place, and after looking in one direction
and another, dreading lest some should frown upon
him—they were so well dressed he thought they
would not want his company—he at last turned
away into a corner, and as you looked upon him
you felt glad that you were not such as he. And
you had a right to be glad. It would not be much
to your credit if you were not. But if your thought
did not recognize God as the giver of all that you
enjoy, you had no right to take that gladness and
bind it up with your religion as an offering to God.
Well, so this Pharisee looked upon the publican, and
at once he thought of extortioners, of unjust men,
and of men dangerous to domestic peace, and he
attributed all these qualities to his fellow-worshipper,
and he felt glad in his soul that he was not such a
man. And that was all there was of it; but he called

it thanks to God, and in that he was wrong. Now, it is not uncommon for simple gladness to be mistaken for thanks to God. A man may be glad for a good harvest, because his home is bright and happy, because his sons are prospering in business, or his daughters are happily married, and all are well, and it is right to be glad for all such things. An infidel is as glad from all such causes as a Christian is; but it is very likely that his thought is that his own skill and shrewd management have brought all this about, while the gratitude of a truly devout heart recognizes God as the giver of everything that causes the heart to be glad.

And so, wearied of his acquaintance, we will leave that Pharisee at his devotions and with his God.

We turn now to the rude publican, who stands in the dark shadow of the portico, and scarcely dares allow his voice to be heard, while with much abasement of self, he prays simply, "God be merciful to me a sinner."

He is an example of the manner in which we ought to come to God. Let us study this example for our guidance.

1. The first noticeable thing is his forgetfulness of everything but himself and God. There is no thought of how he may appear in the eyes of other men. He is entirely indifferent to the ill opinion formed of him by his fellow-worshipper, the Pharisee. God is there, and it is He whom he would reach. It is not for me to say how often it may occur that

people come into the temple more concerned as to
the appearance they shall have in the eyes of other
men than in the eye of God. This humble man,
taught only by the Spirit, is a guide to all.

2. Then we learn that in a successful prayer we
must recognize what we are. "God be merciful to me
a sinner." This man was a sinner. He felt it, he
acknowledged it. He built not upon boasted virtues
either of his ancestors or of himself. There was no
ostentatious leading in of deeds of charity. And
yet, I doubt not, this man had had his good thoughts,
and felt many a noble and generous impulse,
and had done some good deeds in his life. One day
he had been on his rounds, collecting the taxes for
his employer, and he came to a poor vinedresser's.
The year had been a bad one, and the poor man had
not his money ready, so the publican with many
bitter words seized all the fruit he could find—some
bundles of figs, and some baskets of grapes and
oranges. As he turned away he heard the poor man's
hungry child cry out for some figs, and it touched
him. On he went toward the place of deposit, and
in the distance he saw a lonely figure upon the high-
way. It was a leper. He had just been declared
by the priest hopelessly infected, and the usual
ceremony had just taken place. The burial service
was read over him, a shovel of earth thrown upon
him, and so all his kindred were taught to think of
him as one among the dead. He had been turned out
alone, and as he came along his sad voice sounded

doleful enough, as according to law he laid his hand upon his lips, and cried out, "Unclean, unclean!" The publican saw and heard him. The cry of the vinedresser's child had touched a tender chord in his heart, and it vibrated afresh when he saw the suffering leper, so he did what many better men would not have done. Gathering up a bundle of figs and a branch loaded with the best oranges, and several large clusters of grapes, he ran forward and threw them hastily at the feet of this leper to whom no one was permitted to give food. That night after all the hard acts of one of his worst days, he went to his den, and sitting alone reflected. His manner of life seemed damnable in his own eyes. His better instincts told him that he was at war with both God and man. In his thought he said, "It has come to my knowledge that Curtius paid half a million sesterces for the taxes of Judea, and he is trying to collect one and a half millions. It is too much. He has already grown enormously rich by driving such bargains; but such money must be anathema. And it is by such instruments as I that he is enabled to rake in his enormous gains. I get the odium, he gets the money. I will not do it any longer. To-morrow I will go to him and throw up my district." This man had sincerely desired, and earnestly tried to do better. But what can an unaided man do against all hell, and all of his own world? This man felt that he could not do much, so he determined to try another way, and come to God. I don't believe any of his good thoughts or acts were valueless in the sight of God. I don't believe any good that any man ever does will be lost; but when he opened his lips in prayer, he made no mention of any good thing he had ever done. He only remembered that he was a sinner.

So we all, when we stand in God's presence, must remember only that we are sinners in His sight. How else shall we go? Shall we claim that we are naturally good? Then the testimony of all who have ever lived will cover us with confusion, as it declares that "there is none good, no, not one," and asserts that we were "shapen in iniquity, and conceived in sin." Shall we claim that we are not personally guilty? Out of the living word shall flame against us the testimony, that "all have sinned and come short of the glory of God." "If we say we have no sin, we deceive ourselves, and the truth is not in us. If we say we have not sinned, we make Him a liar, and His word is not in us." Shall we come claiming that by a life of strict purity continued for a long time we have made ourselves acceptable to God? Why, no matter how long we may, if it were possible, obey every commandment, still that makes no provision for the sins we committed before our life of strict obedience commenced.

3. We pass on now to learn a third lesson from this humble man as to the right manner of approaching God. We notice what he sought. He prayed for mercy. Now, what could be so appropriate to the

case of a sinner as mercy ? Granting all his good deeds, still they did not rise so high, nor were they so numerous as to justify him in asking a reward for them. Imagine any man among us going to God asking to be rewarded for the goodness of his life. Select the holiest man or woman from any church, and think of the impression that would be made upon your mind, if he should go up to God and claim a reward for any work done in this world ! Such a fancy shows us how very much out of the way such a petition would be. No one has done anything for which he may claim a reward. If it is all of grace that a man is saved, or taken into heaven at all, much more it is of grace that any value is attached to his good deeds, and any measure of happiness allowed to him in consequence of them ! He may receive such reward as an undeserved gift, but may not claim it as a just compensation.

Again, if a sinner should ask for justice, the first gift it presented would destroy him. But one thing remains which he can ask, and that is, mercy. Nothing else is suited to a sinner. But there is a deeper meaning to this prayer for mercy than appears on the surface. This will come out in an enquiry as to the conditions upon which the suppliant expected to receive mercy.

There are three ways by which sin may be disposed of without punishing it with death.

The first which I will mention is simply letting it go as if it had never been committed. The idea of disposing of all sin in this way has been growing in popularity during the last few years. Books have been written in favor of a plan so simple. Churches have been built up on this idea as a foundation stone. Many, in their zeal for the adoption of such a method, have appeared to denounce any system of theology which provides for the adequate punishment of sin. To-day the man who dares use the words "eternal punishment" to express what he thinks sin deserves, will expose his popularity to great risks. Now, on this subject several things may be said.

The first is, that this letting sin go, just as if it had never been committed, and saying nothing about it, is a plan which has never been adopted by men to any great extent in their dealings with each other. But few persons will let offences against themselves pass unnoticed. Even good men find reasons sufficient to justify them in exacting an account for every deed done against them—such as their own dignity, the good of society, the best interests of the offender himself. Oh, there are just grounds enough why a man should seek redress for all affronts. If it be a simple debt that can be cancelled by money, the very principles upon which good business men conduct their affairs would be perverted and strangled, if a creditor should just let a debt go as if it had never been incurred. For other offences the method of shooting the offender is not so common as it once was, but still in some way men continue to demand reparation for all the sins committed against them-

selves.   It is only the sins committed against God
that they are so anxious to pass over without any
notice.

But the fact is that sins committed against God
do not touch everyone, and all whom they do not
touch can easily manage to let them go as if they
had never been committed, but the same persons grow
furious and unrelenting in their demand for instant
redress if one of these offences chances to cut into
their lives or plans. No, this simple method of just
letting an offence pass without notice will never
become popular among men as a mode of dealing
with each over.

Another thing that may be said upon this subject
is, that this plan has never been taught to be God's
method in dealing with the sins of transgressors.
No religious system has ever taught mankind that
their offences against the Deity would be good-
naturedly passed over as if no offence had been
given. Both heathen and Jewish religions have
been full of bloody sacrifices for sin. Nor yet is
there anything in the history of nations from which
men would get the idea that sin is so small a matter
that God will just pass it over in good nature,
as a man passes over his child's or brother's hasty
word. In all ages history and religion have united
to impress the human mind with the idea that sin
will be followed with terrible punishments. Cain
was banished. Achan was stoned. Every Jew
either experienced the extreme penalty of his sins,

or else he saw a sacrifice bleed upon the altar as an atonement. Among all heathen nations the punishments of sin against the gods were bloody and terrible.

Now, it is safe to say that this publican knew enough about the shedding of the blood of both Jewish and heathen sacrifices, to prevent any expectation arising in his mind that his sins would be forgiven without an atonement. He did not pray for any such exhibition of mercy. He did expect that good nature would overlook as of no consequence the sins which he himself felt to be exceeding sinful, and would forget offences which he himself could not forget. Now, under such circumstances can you think of a man offering a prayer that would not in some way recognize an atonement? Imagine a Jew or Gentile standing in the temple, literally reeking with blood, and praying for mercy without any recognition of a bloody atonement! Why, it would be impossible. A man in that age could not get hold of such an idea. He could not think such a thing. Everything was forcing into his mind the notion of atonement for sin by blood, and it was not possible for him to think of mercy coming in any other way.

This, then, was what the publican meant when he called for mercy. He did not expect that the Almighty, in answer to his prayer, would amiably let his sins pass as if they never had been committed, but his soul was pierced with the thought, how

great is my need of an atonement! Who of all the
thronging multitudes, so needy as I! O that a
sacrifice were offered in my behalf! O that I also
might escape from death on account of my sins, by
a sacrifice being offered for me! O God be merciful
to me a sinner! O God let an atonement be found in
my behalf! I have no offering to bring, but let me
not be unatoned for and unforgiven! Let there be
a propitiation for me also!

Now, this is the meaning of the publican's prayer.
It was a prayer for propitiation. It was his earnest
cry for Christ.

I have, by various steps in my argument, shown
that the spirit of the age in which the publican
lived, the ideas that filled the air around him, would
lead him to embody in his prayer a petition for an
atonement. But now I come to the stronger point
that this meaning is distinctly contained in the word
itself which he used.

The third way of getting sin out of the way
without the death of the sinner is by a satisfactory
atonement, which preserves the authority of the
law which has been broken, and yet makes it possible to let the sinner go free. Now, the publican
had this plan of escape in his mind. Never in his
life had he seen anything in the customs of men
that would suggest any other way to his thought.
Both heathen and Jewish altars were constantly
drenched in blood. Its ever-flowing stream taught
men the great evil of sin. If the blood of the sacri-

fice did not 'flow, then the blood of the offender must flow. He had seen men bringing their animals to offer in sacrifice. He had seen the priests standing at the holy altar offering the sacrifices for the people.

The word translated "merciful" means first a propitiation, an atonement; then, as pardon or the showing of mercy followed the offering of atonement, the word had a secondary meaning, and that was "merciful." The word in the original Greek is ἱλάσθητι, from ἱλάσκομαι. Now, we find this same word in Homer, and we may safely take it for granted that he knew the proper meaning of Greek words, and if we can get a clear idea of what he means by the word, we may put that meaning into this passage.

In one place Homer represents the Greeks as suffering from the ravages of a plague, which they believe was sent upon them from Apollo, in anger on account of an offence which they had committed against him. They had carried a virgin as a captive away from the service of his temple. A wise counsellor among them, Chalcas, advises that, to make amends for the offence they had committed, they should return that virgin to the temple, and then offer to Apollo a hecatomb as a bloody sacrifice. He encourages them to hope that the god, being thus propitiated, will turn aside their calamity. Now, the word which Homer uses to describe the effect of that sacrifice is the same which is here used in this prayer. Apollo will be propitiated, he will have mercy. It follows, then, that any proper regard for correct interpretation will compel us to see in this man's prayer an appeal for an atonement. Let God be propitiated in my behalf! Let a Messiah, a Christ, be found for me!

Now, in this he is a singularly striking example to us of what we need when we come to God. We need Christ only, always, and supremely. We must come with the persuasion that there is no salvation for us but in Him.

What we, as sinners, need to pray for is Christ, just as this poor publican prayed for Him. It is in vain that we pray for mercy, except as it is provided for by His death. But if we pray for mercy through His name, and trust to the merits of His sacrifice, then for His sake all our sin may be passed over; and the divine justice will be as much honored and exalted in our forgiveness and salvation as it could possibly be in our destruction as a punishment for our sin.

3. Again, this publican is to us an encouraging example, for " he went down to his house justified." So will everyone who, like him, comes to God in an acceptable manner, with a due recognition of his own sinfulness, and a proper regard to Christ's atoning sacrifice. The humble shall not come to God in vain. No sinner need then despair. If God can pardon sin at all, He can pardon the worst sins, and all the sins of the worst man who ever lived, just as easily through Christ as the sins of the best man who ever lived.

THANKS FOR THE GIFT.

A CHRISTMAS SERMON.

"Thanks be unto God for His unspeakable gift."—2 CORIN-
THIANS ix. 15.

THIS is the one day of all the year for joy and
gladness. Even the grey hairs of the most
aged and venerable shake with the laughter within.
And from that highest snow-crowned peak in all the
area of human life, the ever-increasing stream of
laughter goes rippling and sparkling down through
the domestic circle. The maternal brow, marked
with burdens and cares, becomes more placid and
smooth, as the remembrances that each year has
sacredly treasured up in the true heart, pour in a full,
fresh current over the gladdened spirit. The little
stream of laughter on the cold peaks of age becomes a
resistless torrent as it dashes into the nursery, scatter-
ing toys and delicacies in reckless confusion, breaking
out in wild huzzahs and shouts, in triumph that
school laws have lost their jurisdiction, and that the
fragments of the family, scattered for purposes of
business and education, are drawn together again by
the resistless magnetism of love. What a day,

18

that can send clear around the world peals of laughter echoing and answering back, and currents of sympathy that soothe and heal, and make the tears dry more rapidly!

Of all the days of the year, this should be a day of thanksgiving and praise. Whatever doubts may be started as to the 25th of December being the exact date, certainly we do know that the Christmas child came into the bleak wilderness of our world's life, and came as a gift of God so precious that no human language can state how high is the estimation in which it should be held. It is indeed "the unspeakable gift!" And every child knows that it is because of His coming that on this day an anthem of unwritten music, inspired by the deepest feeling and highest and purest emotion of the human heart, floats up to the throne of God in the pealing notes of laughter and joy from millions and millions of happy Christian children!

But how to be thankful, that is the question. Gladness and thankfulness to God are not the same. An atheist is as glad when his health is good and his business prosperous as a Christian can be. But he knows nothing of true thankfulness to God. How can we as Christians raise the gladness of this day up to the higher plane of true, fervent thanks to God for the gift that gives the day its character? A great many Christian people are discouraged because they have not realized from their hard-fought battle in life all they had hoped for. A man sat at

his desk where for a good many hours he had been
bending over his work in intense application. His
mind at last turned in upon itself and refused to
deal with the figures and problems before it any
longer. He threw himself back in his chair and
spread his hands over his face and closed eyes. He
was a man in moderate circumstances in life, and
with increasingly high prices of everything needed
by his family, his efforts had not succeeded in bringing a proportionate increase of income. And as he
sat there wearied in his chair, not asleep and yet
not wholly awake, naturally his thoughts ran on his
worldly condition.

If by some grand speculation he could find a short
road to fortune—if a draft should fall at his feet,
as if from the sky, making him the owner of
millions, how grandly he would use this new wealth
entrusted to his hands! And then his thought flew
abroad, visiting one and another of the many
acquaintances whom his munificence should bless.
His fancy saw boxes of tea and raisins, and barrels
of sugar and flour, and hams and fruits pouring into
the homes of the surprised poor, and of distant
friends whom he knew, all in time for Christmas
festivities; and furs and costly garments, and beautiful books and all manners of toys that delight
children. And as for his own home, it had suddenly
become a richly furnished eastern paradise, where
his wife moved a queen, and his children sat radiant,
happy, and beautiful as if sent from the celestial

spheres. Such glory it was too bad to disturb, but duty sternly called him back to the plain and homely realities of his life. And as he took up the thread of duty he soon became aware that he was less contented than before his gorgeous waking dream. Dwelling in fancy upon grand possibilities had increased his happiness the less in proportion as their realization was grossly improbable!

Here, then, is one point made. Neither thankfulness nor happiness grows while we are comparing ourselves with others. There are two ways of making such comparisons. Those whose worldly endowments are slender may think of them only in comparison with other persons who have much more; but in this way fancy runs up the ladder so rapidly, that no matter how large one's share of gifts and mercies, he would still see some more blest, and in his more advanced condition, his contentment would be poisoned the same as in the less advanced. For this reason no thankfulness will be promoted by comparison. Envy, spitefulness, gangrene, and covetousness are the usual fruits of our dwelling much on other people's prosperity as compared with our own; and, indeed, in ninety-nine cases out of a hundred, discontent does not arise because people have not enough for necessary comfort, but because they have not quite as much as others. They may be beyond the highest point reached by their dreams of prosperity in some previous period of life, but so long as another family is able to pay for higher-priced articles—though the cheaper answers the purpose equally well—they cannot be contented and thankful. They have not philosophy enough to know that fancy prices are invented to gratify the vanity of ignorant people, who happen to own money, and have nothing else.

The other way of making comparison is where a person, by inheritance or success, has gained the whole world—that is, money enough to have, without any anxiety, everything this world can give. Many such persons were brought up in very poor circumstances, and would really be more natural and easy if living as they were always accustomed : but the satisfaction they derive from their possessions comes from knowing that others envy them. Indeed, it is not flattering to human nature to know that the real value of expensive things to their possessors lies, in very many cases, in the fact that many others who cannot afford the same will look upon them with covetous eyes. It is a pitiable spirit ; but human breasts will harbor it. The value of the splendid carriage, and dashing team, and gorgeous apparel, and stately mansion would be greatly depreciated if they awakened nobody's wonder and surprise. Less costly things would serve the place as well and afford as much happiness, but would not reflect so much consequence upon the possessor. Now, persons of this class will find their contentment as much disturbed as poorer people do, if they make comparisons between themselves and others in respect to the consequence they have in others' eyes. Such a person, who had the glory of a trace of the blood of the nobility in his veins, was trying to browbeat a laboring man. The man was silent for a good while. At last he looked up, and with suggestive coolness, uttered these remarkable words: "If thoo knewest how little I care for thee, thoo'est be surprised." It is very suggestive to reflect that to many people the value of great possessions lies in the fact that they make just such people as this plain man care for the one that possesses them. If people would once cease to rate a man's consequence by his money, there would be an end of the discontent that comes from comparing ourselves with others, both among the rich and among the poor.

This was the first truth the weary man learned from his waking dream as he sat in his chair in his office. He was not more happy and contented and thankful for the comparison made in thought between his condition and that of others. But he performed his duties and went home. He found a loving wife and bright, healthy children. They sat together at a plain meal, but rose refreshed, and he thought, "Why, a king's repast could not better satisfy the needs of his body, or give more enjoyment in partaking." Reading that evening, he came upon a little article on domestic economy, and, among other things, it said to him, speaking on means of happiness, "Live within your income."

The article was addressed to persons in much poorer
circumstances than his own, and yet it assumed that
they could in some way keep within their income,
while he had been indulging the thought that he
could not possibly live within his. The next day
his duties called him through some narrow, dark
alleys of the city. He saw there children with
cheeks fresh and rosy, and babes crowing in intense
delight, and mothers bending over them with tender,
yearning love. Especially he saw a plainly dressed
mother and boy enter a car. The boy cared for a
large bundle, and passing a large factory he told his
mother at his side what he had seen one day of
their way of lifting large and heavy boxes to the
highest flat. When they got off, the man saw them
go to a small house back from the street, not very
near to any other, and the boy let his mother in, and
seemed contented to be at home again. "There,"
thought the man, "are happiness and contentment,
because they feel that between them and the very
rich is a great gulf fixed which they do not hope
ever to pass over ; but because I am nearer to the
charmed circle I am miserable and complaining."
In some way, though he could not tell how, before
he entered his home that night a great peace and
sense of comfort and thankfulness had settled down
upon his perturbed spirit like a soft, warm, downy
mantle over a shivering body. He thought of the
great mansions in the city's splendid streets, and
they seemed to him to be furnished chiefly with

great cares. They no longer called forth his envy.
He said to riches, and pomp, and vanity, "If thou
knewest how little I care for thee, thou would'st be
surprised;" and, he added, "I am surprised myself."
He had discovered that every man is a king by
being master of his own circumstances. From that
moment he dreamed no more about short roads to
fortune. Thenceforth the gifts that cheered his
children at Christmas time, though they had less of
gilt and spangle than some which he had left in the
store because of the too high price, yet were
not less valuable. His children's enjoyment of
them, incapable as they were of knowing or caring
that they were not the most costly gifts, covered
them over with a gilding more precious than fine
gold. He had learned to be thankful because he
had learned not to compare his lot enviously with
those more rich and prosperous in this world.

But when he told the experience, he always said
it was the ministry of the blessed Spirit that taught
him how much he owed to God, and how to prize
all that he had received.

Here, then, are two steps gained toward a thankful spirit : Avoid envious comparisons with those
who have greater earthly treasures ; remember the
models of happy contentment among those not so
well furnished as yourself.

But to advance one step more, there is one kind
of comparison which aids gratitude, that is, a comparison between this world's riches and the qualities

of character founded in Christ, for their peace-giving power and for the permanence of their ministry. Any spirit must be of a lower mould, not to sáy mean or base, that can find any considerable satisfaction in awakening other people's envy. Any spirit sensitive to the most refined and delicate sensations must feel that every great success is discounted by the fact that many experience chagrin and vexation because they have not been elected to the same coveted lot. To possess great wealth is to enter an arena where some of the rankest passions of the human heart find their fullest action. There are reasons enough why people will ever desire riches, but among them all you will not find this one, that the highest peace is found with the greatest possessions. But when a man lives in Christ and moulds his character according to His precepts and example, the one thing which he does find is inward peace. Equally in the palace and the cot Christ brings peace to His people. Then as to the permanence of their ministry, the contrast is equally monitory. At all times the richest men are occupied largely in guarding their possessions lest they take wings. If they succeed, what point do they make? Their riches will not show an equal interest to keep their owners.

One year ago last August I went back to the home of my childhood. I remember how narrow had been my world—the world of a country boy. Many a summer day I watched the waggons coming and going until they disappeared from my sight over the

hill, and I wondered where they went to. Sometimes a grand covered carriage would pass along,
with gaily dressed ladies and imposing looking grey-
bearded gentlemen entirely foreign to our quiet
neighborhood, and as I saw them pass over the hill
out of my sight I wondered, with a child's wonder,
where their world was. It was somewhere entirely
outside of my little world, and so far as my fancy
could go they were removed to an infinite distance
from me, and passed our street just as comets sometimes wander within the path of our earth's orbit.
How hard my young thoughts knocked at the doors
of that great world beyond, and tried to realize what
it could be. Did trees grow there, and waters flow,
and hills and valleys alternate after the manner I
was accustomed to see ? And so I watched and
wondered until the years came and went, and at last
told me I must go out into that world, for I was a
boy no longer. When I went back, then, last year
(in 1880), I found considerable changes. A railroad
had cut through the farm and carried me within
arm's length of the crystal spring where so often I
had stooped to drink. A stranger owned the soil
that to me was consecrated by a father's toil. But
the road where I watched the carriage was there
just as of old, only it did not climb a hill any more—
only a slight rise in the ground; and the great distances that taxed a child's ideas and strength were
shrunk into such little spaces. And the people I had
known were not there. In some cases their children,

my schoolmates, stood in their father's stead; but many of these were not there. But the grassy hillside by the church was there, with the rugged path up to it, and was fast becoming crowded with white monuments. And as I stood at the old gateway and looked toward it, and the road steadily narrowed until it seemed to come to a point just at the old church-yard, the distance did not seem nearly so long as once it did. And I thought, no, it is not so far; for all these years I have been running towards it. When I went into it I found where the people were whom I had missed. They had been steadily going one after another through the long narrow road into the silent city. And when I went up into the northeast corner, my father's habitation, the single mound I saw there, when first I visited it many years ago, had multiplied to eight dwellings of my kindred.

Now, I have chosen the country for this picture, because there it is easy to realize how complete a change has taken place in the population in the space of a few years. One's thought can easily sweep the whole length of the street and realize how nearly all the old heads have followed the strange messenger's voice. But what you can perceive in the country is equally true in the city, though you cannot trace it so readily. Truly, then, the ministry of wealth is at best a very short triumph. The failure to gain it ought not to stand in the way of our thankfulness to-day. If the disappointed and the poor, yea, and even the needy ask, "Why should

I be thankful ?   What has the world or Providence
done for me ?"   I say, "Thanks be unto God for
His unspeakable gift."   Christ brings you this day
the forgiveness of sins.   Trust in Him and find a
great and abiding peace for your soul.   Christ
enables you to think hopefully of the child that died
during the year.   It is not lost.

Christ enables you to look out from the windows
that overlook the unknown, with consolation and
hope !   He came to us.   Let us rejoice, if so be that
we trust in Him, that each passing year is hurrying
us along the road that leads to His presence where
there is fulness of joy, and to His right hand where
there are pleasures for evermore.

THE MEMORY OF THE JUST.

OUR study at this time is the effect upon mankind of the enduring memory of a good life;
and I ask you to notice—

I. That the memory of the just or good man
is blessed in the happy impressions left on the
world's memory by goodness, as contrasted with
the impressions left in some other way.

Men have entered into history through different
gates. Some have purchased their throne in the
world's recollection by laying the foundations of an
empire; some by leading a people up out of a condition of fateful bondage, and giving them a system
of righteous laws; some by discoveries and inven-
tions which have vastly enlarged the possibilities of
human comfort and knowledge; and some by the
thoughts they have dropped into the mind of the
race, or the good they have devised for it.

Now, people generally, and more especially children, are likely to regard those alone as great and
noble who are often met walking up and down the
pages of political history. Warriors and statesmen
are the models most frequently placed before the

minds of youth to inspire in them a great ambition. But actually political, or national fame, is not an object to be sought in comparison with goodness in thought and deed. The one may for a brief interval dazzle us as the blazing splendor of a passing meteor; but the abiding impression that is left is as often one of repulsion as of attraction. There is almost always something to dread from encroaching selfishness in such great personages while living; and much that charity teaches us to forget when they are dead; but the memory inspired by goodness asks no shield from charity. One motive to noble deeds furnished to mankind, one act of helpful love performed, is something given to the world for its happiness, and it will reproduce itself, feeding for ages the hunger of the world's heart for a higher life. The children of distant generations will take hold upon it, and brace themselves for a more determined struggle after virtue and truth.

A few summers ago I looked upon two historic monuments—one, the tomb of Napoleon, crowded by curious, wonder-gazing hundreds, the sarcophagus containing the warrior's dust resting under a great dome of gold ever blazing in the Parisian sunshine; all the surroundings suggestive of pomp, and magnificence, and exhaustless wealth. The fancy, even of French artists, could picture nothing grander. The other monument I found in a cemetery in Geneva. It is a small piece of marble—a mere post —not a foot high, on which are engraven two letters only—J. C. Beneath it reposes the mortal part of John Calvin. Do these two monuments actually represent the world's memory of these two great men? No. Napoleon's tomb represents simply the idea of a few statesmen, as to the tribute due to military greatness; but the child, and the woman, and the humble man—all, indeed, who are comprised in the crowding millions of earth, remember Napoleon much as they would remember a storm, sweeping with darkness, and dread, and desolation, and blood, and death in its strong right hand!

But how different the memory of John Calvin! You may gather more than half the Protestant people of the earth, and in some way or other, the memory of John Calvin, by his teaching, enters into all that is best in their lives, and fills and elevates their souls in death! Truly by such a contrast the memory of the just is blessed indeed!

II. We pass to a second thought. The memory of the just is blessed in the perpetuation of their goodness. It is God's plan that evil shall perish, but that good shall endure. The memory of the just is blessed because it shall continue while "the name of the wicked shall rot."

What is most permanent of all that we see or know in the earth? Why, certainly, thoughts, principles, virtues, truth, goodness. I hold before you this book. There are two ideas which the mind may entertain of it. The first is the binder's or the printer's idea of it. That includes just what your eyes see as I hold it before you. It is a book, that is, it is a shape, and is composed of certain material substances, as leather, paper, twine, glue, printer's ink. But this is a very low idea of a book, and according to it one book is about as good as another, for all are pretty much the same. But, now, what is the second idea of a book? Why, the thoughts that are expressed in it—the truth it teaches—the principles it unfolds. This is the only idea that a philosopher, a poet, or any thoughtful reader ever entertains of a book. Its external form is nothing—its teaching is all. Now, according to the first idea, a book may perish. Bring together all the books ever made, all will perish in time, just as Napoleon's tomb will crumble away! But, according to the second idea, a book can never perish. The thought it contains will last forever; but such is all goodness. It is not the material part of a book, but its imperishable teaching! Goodness, then, is that which lives when all material forms perish, and the evil perishes with them. For a time the world trembles under the tread of conquering heroes. But they pass away and men remember little of them but their names. New national boundaries are defined. Systems of laws are re-formed, and the world soon moves on as though these men had never been; but an impression left by goodness in any form spreads and grows like a mountain torrent, with ever-increasing beauty and power. Tamerlane believed that the world should

have but one master, and that he was born to be
that master. Where he won a great battle, there he
reared a pyramid made of the skulls of his enemies.
His greatest monument was such a pyramid containing eighty thousand skulls. He thought himself the hand of destiny, but he has perished utterly
from the face of the earth. Not an institution,
nor a law, of his creation, remains; not even a
boundary marked out by him is now recognized.
But Abel, a humble shepherd lad, brought a lamb
and offered it to God by faith. We have not been
informed of any other work that Abel did, but that
act stood at the beginning of a long contest between
good and evil. In that struggle the clash of arms
shall go on until time shall be no more, and in every
part of it, the influence of Abel's act shall arise.
Not a child shall bow to pray, no humble man shall
strive against his sins, no poor widow offer her mite
to God in faith—but the spirit of Abel's act, in offering an acceptable sacrifice, shall be reproduced, and
the influence of its memory shall be felt.

Voltaire did his utmost to mould the thought of
Europe to sceptical forms, and to fill the heart of
humanity with a more intense hatred against God
and Christ. He wrote many volumes, in not one of
which did he lose sight of this bad ambition. He is
dead, and most of his writings are silent in the
grave of forgetfulness. Few authors so voluminous
have gone out under so general an eclipse, perhaps
none in so short a time; but someone—his name is

not now known—some kind father, or more likely
some tender loving mother, looked upon the face of
her little child, whose flaxen curls were fast drooping
over her arm, as the head sank in weary sleep, and
she thought out a sweet evening prayer, for the
lisping child. There were only four lines, for the
child was weary, and they were natural, and easily
remembered :

> " Now I lay me down to sleep,
> I pray the Lord my soul to keep :
> If I should die before I wake,
> I pray the Lord my soul to take."

Compare those few words with Voltaire's volumes.
There is scarcely a child, over all the world, where
our language is spoken, but feels a gladdening influence in his heart when he repeats those lines,
and as the mother, with dewy eyes, hears them,
bending over the lowly form, she turns away,
feeling like Mary of old, that she has something
inconceivably precious to hide in her heart. Here
again we find that the evil perishes, while the good
endures. It appears to be God's law. The wind
bears a plague into a city. The plague runs its
course and perishes. The people pass through its
sorrows and live in a purer atmosphere, with better
health, for the wind has not perished, but returns
every morning with a message of health, and purity,
and happiness, to the same city's crowding thousands.
Tne evil plague is an accident : the currents in the

air are God's permanent way of working. So is the
divine plan and law that goodness shall live on forever. It returns like the dew-drop that shines
pearl-like on leaf and flower, but soon dries up and,
to the simple mind seems lost forever; but in what
varied forms that dew-drop comes back to us again!
It has helped to paint the tints on the rose which
carries its fragrance into the sick chamber, and to
shape the curved lily that sympathizes with sadness
and tears, as it lies, full of hopeful suggestions, on
the quiet bosom of death : and it looks down upon
us in its glorified form and color from its home in
the rainbow. That dew-drop is typical of every
form of goodness, going out apparently in darkness,
but coming back to us in many ways, forever walking unseen, but never with aimless feet !

III. Let us now pass to another consideration
illustrative of the blessed memory of the just. It is
the fact that goodness is perpetuated, irrespective
of the position the individual occupies among men.

God treasures the graces of the lowly as sacredly
as those of the great.

There was once a licentious, but very powerful,
queen of Egypt. Her beauty gave her power to turn
the legions of the Roman army, and greatly to influence the destiny of that greatest empire the world
ever saw. She is gone, and her name is remembered
chiefly by an obelisk, condemned to stand, of all
places, amid the magnificence of great London, where
on every hand it is overshadowed, and can never

appear but pitiably small, and suggestive neither of
riches nor grandeur. It is correct to say that she
has utterly perished from the earth. Her great
position could not continue to her any measure of
influence.

There was a general in Syria, whose wife had a
little captive maid, and her ministry, simple but true
to God, led a proud man to learn the virtue of hum-
bler ways. As long as a soul stained with the leprosy
of sin shall seek healing at the cross, so long shall the
influence of that humble maid continue to preach
that salvation lies in the paths of humility. While
the great has perished, the humble walks the earth
forever. And how many examples occur to illustrate
that humble goodness is as fragrant with God as the
gifts of the great. Some man—no one knows who
—we only know that it was one of a certain group
of twelve men, felt in his heart the promptings of a
gracious influence which raised him nearer to God,
and caused him to feel the need of special guidance,
and being full of a prayerful spirit he longed to find
some proper means for its expression, and he made
a simple request of the friend more loved and
trusted than any other upon earth. He said, "Lord,
teach us to pray as John also taught his disciples."
That request was answered by the gift of a form of
prayer, which has ever since, more than any other,
expressed the yearnings of the world's heart after
God, and has cast its burdens upon him ; and which
comes to us when we are weary, and when we are

THE MEMORY OF THE JUST.

sick, and when we are not strong enough to control
our thoughts, and in such times it gives a voice to
all that our hearts can think or desire! What a
blessing has attended the memory of that disciple's
goodness, which resulted in that simple request!

The mightiest power the world has ever felt
began in simple, unpretending, unknown goodness!

Rome is a name signifying *strength*. The Greek
word *rhomé* literally means strength. When the
power of her victorious armies was the only power
known anywhere on earth, and when under the
tread of her invincible legions, the world was
trembling in fear, there was a child of humble
parents, in a despised village of Galilee, who, by the
force of his goodness and love, was to become
mightier than all the legions and pomp of mighty
Rome. Though Herod, the ruler of the province,
tried to destroy that helpless and harmless child,
yet he lived to reach maturity, and was then put to
a malefactor's death, in the reign of Tiberius, under
sentence of one Pontius Pilate. All these are now
gone, Herod, Tiberius, Pilate, Jesus. Once in a while
the names of the first three are now mentioned, but
only that men may turn away from them with a sick-
ening and pained sense of shrinking horror ; but the
name of the obscure child is hourly in the minds
of uncounted millions, the source of the brightest
joys that gladden men's hearts in life, and the
foundation of the most enduring hopes that in death
take hold upon immortality !

These thoughts have irresistibly taken possession of my mind while I have dwelt, as you all have, upon the falling of some marked figures in our church.

In the autumn, William Gooderham had grown weary one evening on his way home from work, and the chariots of the Almighty met him and took him up, and relieved his weary feet of their burden, and before we thought of the meaning of it all, he was at his Father's house and found the door open awaiting his return.

We had not become accustomed to the silence that had come down upon his place when other visitations called others from the songs of earth up into the praises of heaven.

One week ago to-day, William Beatty stood reading the hand-writing upon the seventy-fifth milestone of life's uneven way, when suddenly the light from the way before him shone upon him with such brightness that his charmed eye led him until he found his place among the marshalled hosts of the waiting stars! He was a member of the Metropolitan Church, a quiet, humble, unpretending, honest, good man, who had no claim upon me for any word in this place, except the friendship I felt for him, and the happy memory of delightful association with him, both in and out of the church.

The Rev. Dr. Williams, one of the General Superintendents of our Church, lingered longer in contemplation of the Beulah land that lifted and shifted

its attractive scenes before his waiting eye. After
the last General Conference he took up his loved
burden of labor, and started off on the run, as if he
had felt that a certain distance must be made before
he was overtaken by some malignant pursuer. His
foot seemed a number of times to be caught in the
race, but a year ago the pursuer unmistakably laid
hand upon his shoulder. For a time they kept on at
an even pace, step by step, but it soon became evi-
dent that for the first time in his life he was not
leading but being led. Oh, that long hard race for
the goal ! While the joys of the Christmas season
were going out to meet everyone, he gave up the
contest and reached out his enfeebled hand for help
ere he should fall upon the way. His Saviour took it
into His own, and led His servant up to his place of
rest among the blessed ones.

He was pre-eminently a *true* man. He had not
enough of worldly wisdom to be willing, after the
political fashion, to use any means of leading men to
his point of view, justifying artifice by the reflection
they will be satisfied and glad when once they get
there. He was particular about the methods and
means employed, as well as about the ends he aimed
at. His integrity was so bold and so manifest, that
to put it under any suspicion would have been the
keenest wound that could possibly be inflicted upon
him.

With him religion was a flame. He had known
its deepest experiences. Conscious, present, personal,

and full salvation from sin was the gospel which he lived.

He was a deep thinker and a wide reader, entering with ready delight any and every field from philosophy to chosen fiction; but with it all he had never discovered in himself any variation from the doctrinal standards of Methodism, nor any need for a variation from its rules. Yet he was in no sense a bigot, nor narrow. His world was wide enough to allow to all shades of opinion a field to labor in, and his heaven rich enough to afford a heritage to all who so love our Lord Jesus Christ as to forsake and deny all sin for His sake, through whatever path of truth they might approach the doors.

His life was devoted to the culture of goodness, and his record remains. It shall live in the hearts of those whom he influenced towards goodness, and in the eternal principles he championed, which, reinforced by his word and example, will continue to walk the earth forever.

A distinguished figure has stood among the laity of the Methodist Church, known over all of Canada and in foreign lands, and for more than thirty years one of the most potent factors in all the councils of the Church. With a wide knowledge of men, and intimate acquaintance with the excellences of all other churches, he recently told us in a form worthy of permanence, how in his comparative youth he came to make the Methodist Church his own.

When last week the Hon. John Macdonald died, a strong and most important lever in the machinery of Methodism was broken.

He was a Methodist—but he was more. He was a Christian man for all Christians to own and acknowledge. His views made every man his brother, as was beautifully illustrated in the results of his last long journey—his visit to Alaska last summer. It is our pride at this time to say, that being a Methodist, there was not an existing church with a well known organization but had some experience of his bountiful hand.

He gave to all churches; and all charities, in his own city or out of it, were felt by him to be his own.

He was among men a just and honest man, and no more true than kind. The verdict of this city and this Dominion over his new-made grave will be that he was a good man.

As a Christian he was a consistent man, presenting a proper balance between experience and duty. The consistency and honesty of the balance-sheet joined hands with the great heart of philanthropy and the open hand of general benevolence. So Christ lived in his life, and will live with his enduring memory, and his never-ceasing life-work

ADDRESS

W HEN my Conference appointed me to the duty of this hour, I at once began to question why such an institution as fraternal delegates should exist at all. They take up much valuable time. The best answer I found to my question was that the churches do not propose to leave to the politicians alone the regulation of the relations which shall exist among the great Christian nations.

The politician asks, When, if ever, shall the United States and Canada be organically one nation? He scarcely looks or thinks beyond that point. But the Christian churches say the United States and Canada are already one in all things concerning which it is of the most vital importance that they should be a unit. In the blessed fellowship and service of the truth there is but one thought between us. To make this whole continent Christian and free and great, and to lay its Christian hand upon the peoples throbbing with vice, and crime, and

passion and pain in heathen lands—this is the one
article of perpetual union between the United States
and Canada.

Therefore, looking upon my duty here in the light
of one link in this holy connection, I felt that I
could so far overcome my diffidence and my sense
of the value of your time as to dare to stand before
you.

A second question, certainly very important to me
personally, was what I could say worthy the occasion. I cherish some little hope from the fact that
you cannot know many things which are of the
greatest interest to us. About ten years ago Joseph
Cook said in an interesting prelude that the average
citizen of this great republic does not know that
anything has occurred in Canada since the confed-
eration of the provinces. Now, we are neither
surprised nor jealous that this should be the case.
Indeed, it could hardly be otherwise. You are
many and great. We are few. We have sense
enough to know the difference between fifty or sixty
millions and five or six millions. We can see that
New York and Chicago are greater than Montreal
and Toronto. We need not be told that our material wealth is only a child's purse compared to the
opulence which here rivals the growth of a thousand
years in other lands ! Why should you take much
interest in our doings ?

Our little moon sees the sun, but it may well be
doubted if the great soaring sun as much as knows

that our earth has any moon at all! And so it is
natural that from across your northern boundary
we should see all you do, and just as natural that you
should not know all we do.

Also, the great events in your history are conspicuous, and read by all the world. Our own have
little interest for any but ourselves.

When you had half as many people as we now
have you made the Revolution of 1776 one of the
mightiest facts of history, and thereby your patriots
were lifted so high that, ever since, like snow-
crowned peaks they have been seen from afar, and
like books read by all mankind.

But who knows anything about Canada's little
war sixty-one years later, in which we, too, wrested
from that same Britain's strong hand what is called
responsible government, and so reached the goal of
as perfect political freedom as any independent
State enjoys.

Then again in your war of emancipation, by
statesmanship and by great generalship, the time
was made a glorious era, and your heroes became
their own monuments, known everywhere, and
never to be forgotten.

But who knows anything about the abolition of
slavery in Canada? Why, it was seventy years
before Lincoln's immortal proclamation. It pre-
ceded the great open movements in the British Empire toward the same end. Canada's first parliament consisted of sixteen men. The State-house, in

which they assembled, was a log hut in old Newark, within hearing distance of Niagara's everlasting roar. The wilderness stretched before and all around them. No might was known which could bring it under subjection but the might of the human arm. Negroes were then held in slavery in the province. But thus situated these sixteen back-woodsmen bravely enacted that every slave then in Canada should be free, and that human bondage should be henceforth forever illegal in the province. It was an obscure and now almost forgotten deed, and is scarcely recognized in the grand story of freedom, and is only as one line across the page compared with the records of your gigantic struggle. But was it not grand? Who dares say that God did not use that little fact in some way to help out the results of your great war?

And so it is all the way down the page. Your record has won the applause of the world : ours is not read and little known outside our own borders, but it is inspiring to ourselves. We see nothing in it to be ashamed of. And we find courage in the persuasion that one man can have as much of the favor of God as twenty men, and our inferior num-bers and wealth will not leave us weak if He smiles upon us, as upon you.

And so we do not look toward you with any jealousy. We all sincerely rejoice in your wonder-ful successes; we hold your institutions in the highest respect, for indeed we have copied the most of them. We universally entertain only the most friendly feelings toward the people of this great nation. They who from twenty to twenty-five years ago felt differently do not care to be reminded of it now, and even then, as I very well know, they did not offer all the prayers, no, not by thousand thousands, that Canada offered for the issue of your war.

In this connection we wish you to understand our attachment to the British Empire. I fully recognize that my duty here is fraternal, and not political; but we read such marvellous things about ourselves in United States newspapers, that I can hardly forbear a few words on Canada's political relations. Since coming here I have read, in what I should judge to be one of New York's most sober papers, a long article urging that the annexation of Canada be made a plank in the platform of one of the great political parties. Now, it is none of my business what ends any of your parties aim at; but the reasons urged for this particular course were so remarkable that I must say, that if Canada is not now, or if it never shall be, a part of the United States, the reason is not because we indulge any unfriendly feelings toward this nation. It is not because we feel toward you that we could not live with you and share with you ; but there are other strong reasons. To begin with, we have been brought up to a British connection, and so we are bound to it by all the prejudices of education.

Then, as a matter of political philosophy, we like the British Constitution better than any other. We see it to-day holding liberty by the hand in nearly all the self-governing States of Europe. We know that it serves us well. Under it we are as perfectly free and independent as are the citizens of this republic. There is not one particular in which our liberties, civil or religious, would be advanced by our becoming an integral part of this great nation.

Then, like yourselves, we have a written Constitution in the "British North American Act," which is a practical application in detail of the British Constitution to our circumstances, and conserving those liberties without which Anglo-Saxons cannot live. So that we are made secure that the hand of the British Government will not enter purely Canadian affairs except in the appointment of our Governor-General, and we are practically an independent State. Now, we honestly think that we do better to have our affairs wholly in our own hands than we would if we should engage in a scramble at Washington, not only with ourselves, as now, but with all the other States of this vast Union.

But we are constantly reading that our growing national debt is driving us into bankruptcy. Well, we don't know it. So long as our credit enables us to enter the markets of the world and negotiate loans at the lowest rates, and we are able to meet the accruing interest at a low rate of taxation as compared with our nearest neighbors, we are not going seriously to talk about bankruptcy.

I do not say what our future destiny may be. I know not. But one thing I am absolutely certain about, and that is that we will never be starved into a union with the United States or any other land. We have learned too much independence ever to say that we have found the business of running Canada a failure, and that with bankruptcy staring us in the face, we would like someone to take the business off our hands.

But we are told that we would at once rise into greater prosperity if we were a part of the United States. We do not see how. Our manufacturers and farmers and miners think that they are developing all the wealth our circumstances admit of, as rapidly as men can do it, and as fast as is being done in the States nearest to us. And, as to booming our population, not a man of you would come among us if we were a part of this republic, unless he could make more money there than here ; and, if he could make more money, he would come just as we are. So that, as we look upon the case, our British connection rests upon other reasons than unfriendliness toward you. We do not propose to fight you with men clothed in British red. That has not proved a healthy experiment in the past. But from a business point of view we think our interests may remain as they are.

But there is more than this in our British connection. It gives us a sense of national dignity, or, if you will, it gratifies our vanity. And, after all, what on earth is so persuasive as that which exalts a person's or a people's sense of their own consequence? Now, seeing that our greatness and glory are mostly in the future, we must have some glory to live upon as we go along ; and, being such as we are, I think you will admit that, if we are going to live on glory at all, we require to draw a great deal from abroad. So we draw from it two sources—from Britain's past and from yours. We place all of Great Britain's history behind ourselves, and claim as our own all her victories with pen and sword. We are a part of one of the old empires of history, and so we join hands with antiquity. Magna Charta and the Commonwealth are ours. And William Pitt, and the Duke of Wellington and Waterloo, and all the wealth of storied grandeur in Westminster Abbey, its glory of poetry and history and statesmanship, and all the military pomp that slumbers in mute admonition to the ages in St. Paul's—are not these, and more, ours by inheritance, for are not we, too, Britons ?

Then we turn round and take to ourselves a reflection from the glory of your great achievements also, for are we not Americans ? If we do not shout as you over 1776, still we would neither suppress nor depress your rejoicing. We do not pretend to think that Great Britain has been always right. We waste no admiration upon the King George who

20

ruled at Westminster. But our eyes, as well as yours,
see the grandeur of him whom nature made a king,
though uncrowned. God Almighty's King George
gave his name to the capital of this republic.

Why, we are regularly taught to associate that
name with the highest virtues. Within a month, in
glancing over a work placed in the hands of our
advanced students, I found such expressions as,
"The great hero, Washington," and "The brave and
virtuous Washington." And that work has an origin
as British as a book can possibly have. We also
venerate with you the God-anointed Lincoln and
the invulnerable Grant; and Vicksburg and Gettys-
burg and the Wilderness are glorious in our eyes as
well as in yours.

Why, the fact is, our feelings and interests are so
common with yours, that we are in danger of growing egotistical if you ever talk to us about yourselves. A conceited egotist asked my bright little girl
for her photograph. She promptly replied that she
would give him a looking-glass, for she knew that
would please him better. Well, I come to speak to
you of Canadian affairs and of Canadian Methodism. The conceit and the egotism are, of course,
eliminated from this problem, and I reply to you
that I can only give you a looking-glass in which to
see your own affairs and your own Methodism.

We have the same origin with you ; we speak the
same language, have the same free schools, the same
Christianity, and, to drop to a lower line, we are

moved by the same ambitions; we have the same
Fisheries' Treaty, and, as a Western orator said, we
have the same whiskey; but I say this with a
graver meaning than he did.

Our people are thinking about the same things as
yours. How to get rich by speculations in the stock
exchange, and in real estate or by contracts with the
Government; how to own the earth and then take
the first circles of so-called society by storm. The
laborer studying the most formidable combinations
against capital, the members of each political party
trying to score a point against the other, each
bidding for the laborer's vote and the Roman Catholic vote, the temperance vote and the whiskey vote.
And to all this, and through it all, the flaming
message of godly men and women in sermon and
song and testimony, calling to a holy life here and a
glorious heaven hereafter. Does not this seem to
you more like looking into a mirror than examining
a photo?

But, especially standing before this Conference of
the great Methodist Episcopal Church, in the name
and by the merit of another Methodist Church
whose salutations I have the honor to bring to you,
hearing your discussions, and noting the subjects
engaging your attention, I do not feel like a
stranger, nor do I find any dividing line between us.
The life and work and conditions of our Church are
essentially the same as in yours. These two
churches, with their common sympathies, and with-

out any rivalries, might be organically one, and there would be no difference from the present so far as our practical work is concerned. The likenesses appear at all points, the differences at but few. We labor among people in the same conditions. We have a common Church history. We have the same doctrines, and in substance the same discipline and hymnology, the same itinerant system, the same flitting evangelists, the same holiness controversies, the same ambitious Roman Catholicism to confront, and the same forms of sin to defy and overcome.

If for no other reason, our origin and history give us some claim to recognition here, for we are your eldest daughter. About one hundred years ago your wandering star, William Losee, entered Canada and founded Methodism. The following year another and greater was duly appointed to help carry on the fast enlarging work. And there comes in a pathetic and romantic story of old-time Methodism. These two pioneers were both smitten with the beauty and grace and moral excellence of the same early Canadian maiden. The second comer won the day. The disappointment was disastrous to him to whom we owe so much. And our chroniclers do tell that, in those most interesting records on the face of the earth—the Minutes of the Conference—Dunham and the country appear again, but Losee never. I drop a tear for him, but I am glad the country did appear again in your records. In those early days we meet such names as Martin Ruter and Nathan Bangs. Indeed, a great part of these foundations he was.

And the great Asbury nearly lost his life in making an Episcopal visit to Canada. He was accompanied by the late centenarian, Henry Boehm, and they crossed the St. Lawrence in a novel way. Three canoes were tied together, and, as Boehm relates, there were three canoes, three passengers, three horses, and four Indians. After a fortnight of arduous toil, he crossed the lake under sail, and the record of the voyage might be laid beside Paul's voyage to Rome, so far as its thrilling experiences and its narrow escape are concerned. But the fact I want to impress is that the good Asbury liked us Canadians. Boehm wrote, "The Bishop was delighted with the people," and he wrote: "Here is a decent, loving people; my soul is much united to them." We trust that you feel toward us in the same way still. I know that those are just the feelings we entertain toward you.

You felt a deep interest in the subject of Methodist Union in Canada. You perhaps desire to know how a union of four bodies has worked. What have I to say on the subject? Nothing. We talk at funerals, but not over men in perfect health and full of activity. Their deeds speak for them. It is only breaks and failures that make a great noise. If in practical working our union had been a failure, I would need hours to explain; but, instead, it has been steadily, quietly at work. It took effect in 1884. Our last minutes show that in three years we have added twenty-five per cent. to the membership which came into the union. No, I need not say anything about that union. There it is. Look at it.

This membership is very unevenly distributed over the provinces. The highest percentage to the population is in Ontario. There we have between thirty and thirty-one per cent. of all the people. In the Eastern Provinces we have between twelve and thirteen per cent., and in Quebec, the stronghold of the most formidable Romanism in the world, we have only between three and four per cent.

Reliable statistics four years ago placed before us the encouraging fact that we have more Sunday-schools, and more teachers in them, and, by upward of fifty thousand more scholars attending them than all the other Protestant churches combined.

When we want evidence that Methodism in Canada is a business success, we turn especially to our book and publishing interests. In this respect, in the pages scattered abroad, in the number of hands employed, in the steady advance made, and in the dividends from actual profits fairly earned, annually devoted to our benevolent funds, we feel that for our number, we are not behind the foremost of the great brotherhood of Methodist publishing houses, and we are one with you in the great work of the world's evangelization.

When you, with more than 2,000,000 members,

undertook to raise $1,000,000 for missions, we, with about 210,000 members, undertook to raise one quarter as much as you. You succeeded, and we fell short of our hopes. We have only reached about one dollar per member for missions throughout our whole Dominion. We feel the disordered pulse of heathenism among the native Indians, where at least ten thousand in the North-West are under our influence, and in Japan, the only point we have yet touched in the distant world—a mission that has been a great inspiration to our people. Our Woman's Missionary Society has married it, and the effect is a great awakening of thought and zeal, especially among our young people, until this Woman's Missionary Society, directed by a high degree of consecrated intelligence and wisdom, is really one of the mighty forces of our land.

I mentioned some of the obstacles which confront us. Among these is the most aggressive Romanism in the world. It dominates one province and is ponderous in at least two others. Its artful ambition practises on the politician. In this it rarely fails, and generally, when it does, it is in going too far. A friend related that he was visiting one of our reformatories, and asked a boy of about fourteen for what crime he was confined. The reply was, "For stealing a saw-mill, sir; and I would not have been caught, either, only I was fool enough to come back for the dam." Well, Romanism, generally comes back for the dam. She wants all, and so sometimes she is arrested. There have been a number of instances of this in our past history. The results of Protestant missions in that province, although not indicating failure, yet do not declare a brilliant success.

I quoted some one as saying that we have the same whiskey as you. This is too sadly true. Our Methodism is well-nigh unanimous in the temperance work. Nor have we anything to complain of in the other Protestant churches, nor yet even in the Roman Catholic Church. We sometimes think we are getting the thing pretty well tied up, but we have not yet got a close back-hold upon it, and fear that we will have to wait for perfect victory until God shall chain the old serpent for a thousand years. In this conflict we are learning from your experiences, and with us, as with you, George Haddock's soul goes marching on.

In other respects we have much to encourage us in relation to public morality. We have a quiet Sabbath. There is not one Sunday newspaper in Canada. We have no theatrical exhibitions on the Lord's day. But we have sense enough to know that this immunity is due to the absence of the vast European population which throngs in nearly all your great cities. American families here are, no doubt, as particular in the observance of the Lord's day as the people of Canada are.

We think that moral interests with us have gained strength by the voting of women. It is a fact that women by the thousands do go to the ballot-box in Canada. I have met them there, and have met the same women the evening after in a prayer-meeting, and I can certify that neither their piety nor their modesty was impaired by their contact with a ballot. Indeed, in respect to the effect upon her modesty, I would rather any day see a Methodist lady at the voting-booth than in a ball-room.

I represent here a Methodism conservative both in methods and in doctrine. With special evangelistic agencies at work all around us calling for new adaptations, while we have the most absolute freedom of innovation, we follow the old ways; and we do so only because convinced that they who lived before our time knew some things as well as we know them.

Especially has this persuasion steadied our bark of doctrine in its course through the unrestful sea of change. Canadian Methodism is free from doctrinal agitation; but this does not mean that we are in a condition of either intellectual slumber or moral indifference. Quite the contrary is the truth. But thoughtful men find in their doctrinal standards much greater breadth and depth than we discovered in them when we were probationers. Such persons interpret standards liberally—especially standards so voluminous and varied in character as those of Methodism.

Now that the storms of fierce controversy have

passed away, men of high culture can sit in quietness
and peace, and form an estimate of the finished
works of the mighty men of the past, and then, going
back to the Bible, they discover that it contains
much more than any one man, not excepting even
John Wesley, ever formulated, especially if he
did his work, as St. Augustine and Wesley did,
in the heat of constant, violent controversy.

One result is greater freedom in the statement and
illustration and application of old doctrinal truths ;
not so much regard for the form of words employed,
as for the substance of truth contained in the words.

Another effect is that those who have long stood
apart at wide distances are being drawn together as
by a common impulse, and there are active movements in thought which look toward more striking
unions of ecclesiastical bodies than the world has yet
seen.   As many rivers run into the same sea, so
many reasons move toward the same end.   The
discovery, for example, is being made that sec-
tarianism is a deadly foe to missionary enterprise ;
and that souls may be saved, and even extensive revivals prevail, where Arminianism, at least by name,
is not recognized ; and that through all gates of
doctrine, in some way, in spite of errors, men do find
the cross, and so reach up to a better life.   And
that mere names of systems do not kill, though they
afford fuel for long feuds ; therefore, all that is true
in Calvinism belongs as much to us as to those
churches in which St. Augustine is regarded as a

chief apostle of the truth. And that even our own doctrines, when they have been used as weapons of controversy merely, have been pushed to extremes. In short, that genuine Christian life, like vines, overgrows all the forms set for it to cling to; and strong undercurrents of thought are sure to burst forth in expression.

This is just the stage reached by Christian life and taught in Canada at the present time.

Leading minds in at least three great denominations are speaking out in favor of a consolidation of the three. The way is prepared by a general acceptance of evangelical principles and methods. All our Protestant churches are thoroughly well educated in evangelical ideas. The Baptists are, as everywhere, a spiritual people, and render faithful service to the great body of truth. The Presbyterians are in the front rank in every good work, and they preach a gospel of free salvation to all men, without degrading the sense of Divine sovereignty. The Church of England has, as a rule, an earnest evangelical pulpit, and is heartily active in all moral and benevolent enterprises, and although, as we of course think, she is hampered in method by the traditions which bind her to one set of formalities, yet she does not think so, and she is showing much power of adaptation in the way of missions or revival work. Possibly Canada will yet present to the world the first example of a whole people laying aside all denominational prejudices, and for the love of Christ and men—exalting only the truths essential to salvation, and no longer stirring the bones of the dead in the mouldy mausoleums of the past—who, after all, were only great according to their day and opportunity, and were never called of God to be the mentors of all time.

I rejoice to lay at your feet my Church's tribute of fraternal affection and gratitude. We have learned from your wise example, and have been stimulated by your wonderful successes, and therefore we feel ourselves your debtors. We venerate the shining names which you have lifted up on high. We hold, as in a large sense our own, the men of conspicuous ability who have always adorned that illustrious chair. Up to the present time the majority among us has not favored for our own constant use any dignitary bearing the title of bishop. We call them superintendents, and acute minds among us seem to discern a great difference between being bishoped by a superintendent and superintended by a bishop. But all the same we like the superintendency of bishops so well, that we import yours as often as we can, and every time we love them more. We call them ours, and so they are in all respects except the privilege of voting for them when they are elected. But we go unanimously for whomsoever you may choose. Every successful candidate may consider his majority increased by the number of our whole voting power as a Church. In the years past we have felt your sadness our own, as standing in the shadow cast upon universal Methodism, by the procession of mighty men, who, clothed in the most royal ascension robes, have gone up from that chair, and about it, to their throne in glory. They are to memory as Enochs and Elijahs; for did they not walk with God? Did not their fearless thunder cause the Ahabs of wickedness to tremble? Was there not wider standing-room for truth and righteousness where they shuffled their feet? We catch the inspiration of their luminous example!

Oh, in this grand and awful game of life, all too soon the men disappear from the board! The pawns are lost! The knights are taken! The bishops go, and the queen is seen no more! Our eyes follow them down the fast narrowing path where great forms grow small in the distance! An unseen hand sweeps down upon the board and the game is done! The day strides out over the sea, and the night leaps down from the sky! Yonder the shining gates open wide, and as you bearing your trophies over your heads rush up on one side, we shall crowd in from the other! We extend to you our right hand in the strong bonds of abiding fraternity, and our hearts are with you for a grand triumphal meeting there!

www.ingramcontent.com/pod-product-compliance
Lightning Source LLC
Chambersburg PA
CBHW021214270326
41929CB00010B/1125